GREAT LAKES

LIGHTHOUSES
AMERICAN & CANADIAN

A COMPREHENSIVE DIRECTORY/GUIDE TO
GREAT LAKES LIGHTHOUSES
AMERICAN & CANADIAN

Wes Oleszewski
PHOTOGRAPHY BY WAYNE S. SAPULSKI

AVERY COLOR STUDIOS, INC.
GWINN, MICHIGAN 49841
1998

GREAT LAKES
LIGHTHOUSES
AMERICAN & CANADIAN

A COMPREHENSIVE DIRECTORY/GUIDE TO
GREAT LAKES LIGHTHOUSES
AMERICAN & CANADIAN
Wes Oleszewski
Photography by Wayne S. Sapulski

Copyright 1998
by Avery Color Studios, Inc.

ISBN 0-932212-98-0
Library of Congress Card #98-070577

First Edition 1998
Reprinted 1998, Revised Edition 2000
Reprinted 2002

Published by Avery Color Studios, Inc.
Gwinn, Michigan 49841

DEDICATION

*To my wife Teresa
who is always there for me.*

Shown on the cover: **Seul Choix Point, Lake Michigan**
Established: 1892
Status: Active
Location: (MI) Sixteen miles east of Manistique.
Type: Conical
Access: Car
About the Light: *Similar to the "Poe" style lights of the lakes region, this light resembles Presque Isle, South Manitou, and Au Sable Point. The tower stands 78 feet tall and is made of brick. To access the light you must follow US 2 and exit at Port Inland Road; from there seek County Road 431 to the light. This light is also the site of a museum and gift shop and is run by the Gulliver Historical Society by means of the Michigan Department of Natural Resources.*

TABLE OF CONTENTS

INTRODUCTION

In 1996, Avery Color Studios approached me with the concept of creating a text containing a comprehensive listing of Great Lakes lighthouses. Considering that my normal concentration was in the area of Great Lakes maritime history, such a subject was certainly within the scope of my writing. After all, having written a half dozen books on the shipwrecks of the Great Lakes, Avery thought that I would be the best guide for their readers to visit all of the lighthouses on the lakes. Ordinary "list" books, however, are not really my style, as I prefer to focus on the details of a few select obscure events. I have always thought that the stories of the people and places within the lists are of far greater importance than the lists themselves. Because of my aversion to these simple lists, the shape of this text will be somewhat different from many other books of this ilk. Along with the standard "where" and "when" of these lights, the reader will find some of the fascinating and lesser known facts of the lights and their people.

Some true "light buffs" want to read of every possible illumination device that has ever been erected on or near any waterway. Although such a passion is commendable, such a text would take a decade to assemble and, frankly, could not hold this writer's attention long enough to construct it. Rather, this text will cover the sites that the average folks will visit and admire on the lakes without going into excessive depths of minutia. Most lights reported herein have historic significance and scenic value far beyond a simple range lamp.

Largely, this text is not a first-hand discovery of new-found material with which this author often deals. Rather, it is a gathering of information contained within other sources at hand. Many books of lighthouses cover individual lakes, or regions of the lakes, or selected lights in selected areas. What has been done within these pages has been to take a basket filled with currently published information and compile it into an easy-to-use guide. Sometimes, the currently published material is in conflict. As a result, errors may found be within these pages. Remember, anyone who tells you that he is performing a task without mistakes probably wants your vote. In this case all that I want to do is provide guidance and insight.

Along this path around the lights of the lakes I have been able, in some cases, to use my background in maritime history to provide some interesting tidbits, and a bit of lore that often has no place in my shipwreck books. Also, I have provided an introduction to each lake which will give the first time visitor, as well as the long time resident, a framework and some enticing facts concerning each of the fresh water seas. As this book takes you around the lakes to visit each light you will meet mis-guided explorers, irritable Iroquois, the forgotten inventor of the range light system, brave keepers, ghosts, and much more. I found that a book that was nothing more than a list was just a bit too dull to write, so it was necessary to add some extra fun.

Lastly, it is important to know that although the author of this text has written more than a quarter of a million words on the true adventures of the Great Lakes mariners and shipwrecks, this is my first excursion into the world of the "lighthouse people." It is my hope that this text will be a worthy addition to their efforts to preserve and admire these historic sites. I ask only that the reader will carry with him the thought that I have done my best to create a text that each light buff may use and enjoy in any way that he may see fit. Above all, books such as this should be as fun to read as they are to write.

ABOUT THE GREAT LAKES
LIGHTS IN GENERAL

To most folks who have never visited the Great Lakes, they are simply blue blotches on the map or indigo blobs at the upper right-hand corner of the T.V. weather reporter's fancy computer-animated map. After all, the word "lake" generally refers to a small area of water that you visit on vacation and can look across and see your neighbor's cabin. Such context does not fit the Great Lakes at all. Often, when speaking of these bodies of water, terms of depth are in hundreds or thousands of feet and distances across are in hundreds of miles. Those who are lucky enough to visit or live near the Great Lakes know that they are massive freshwater seas. When you look out across any one of the five lakes, all that you will see is a watery horizon that seems to stretch forever. For the better part of two centuries, these sweet-water oceans have been avenues of transportation of every product that this nation and the Dominion of Canada could consume or produce. The result of the booming of maritime commerce across the Great Lakes led to pressure for the establishment of navigational lights throughout all of the region. By the late 1700s and into the early 1800s, lights were being constructed to warn the mariners of the shoals and shores that could pose a deadly hazard to their vessels. Today, most of the lights that were once so vital to the mariners have been replaced with modern wonders such as radar and the Global Positioning System, or G.P.S. In recent decades, lighthouses have been automated, antiquated and just plain abandoned. Fortunately, societies and organizations sprang up, bent on the preservation of the historic structures that once warned the vesselmen. The lights that our government considered useless are being preserved by a citizenry which is more caring and individuals more far-sighted. Additionally, many of these sites have been converted into tourist attractions and instead of costing money, they are now drawing money into the local community.

Hopefully this book will be a useful guide to these historic aids to navigation and may be a small tool in the job of their preservation. Unlike the saltwater seas, the Great Lakes are a place where names of vessels, lights, captains, keepers and characters are remembered because the community is so tightly related. The lakes may be vast, but the family of their residents is close. Additionally, due to the large concentration of vessel traffic in the mid 1800s, lighthouses are located in close proximity. It is therefore possible for the tourist to visit several sites in a single day and dozens in single vacation. Although many of the lights are located in remote areas that are more accessible to seagulls than to vacationers, many more are as close as a road-side turn off and offer museum facilities to boot. To all who visit these sites, the lights of the lakes should represent a direct link to our past, and a irreplaceable resource of the Great Lakes and the people who reside in this region.

For many decades the industry that was fed by the lakeboats was lumber. The timber-towns of the region produced the product from which America's westward expansion was constructed. When the need for lumber began to decline, there came the steel and auto industries that hungered for the iron ore being shipped from the upper lakes. All of this was heated and powered by coal shipped from the lower lakes. In between those products, grain of all sorts was transported across the lakes. Today, as we watch the decline in Great Lakes heavy industry, a new form of income – *tourism* – is beginning to emerge. Once again the natural resources of the area are earning the money, but now in a passive way. A part of these resources are the many lighthouses located around the lakes. For those who are wise enough, an abandoned lighthouse can become much more than simply an obsolete aid to navigation.

As always, the seasons will change and the Great Lakes will patiently entertain our wishes. In the lumber era the region was clear-cut to point where the land resembled a moon-scape and wild fires swept across enormous portions of the state of Michigan. At one time, the entire upper portion of Michigan's lower peninsula burned from the shores of Lake Michigan to the beaches of

Lake Huron. From the mid 1870s to the mid 1890s, the lakes region was involved in almost continuous forest fires. Today, the clear-cut regions have returned to forested wilderness and you would have to look very hard to find any evidence that the areas had ever been harvested. The lesson: *Man's worst can never outmatch nature's best.* The Great Lakes will always be more enduring than any human effort.

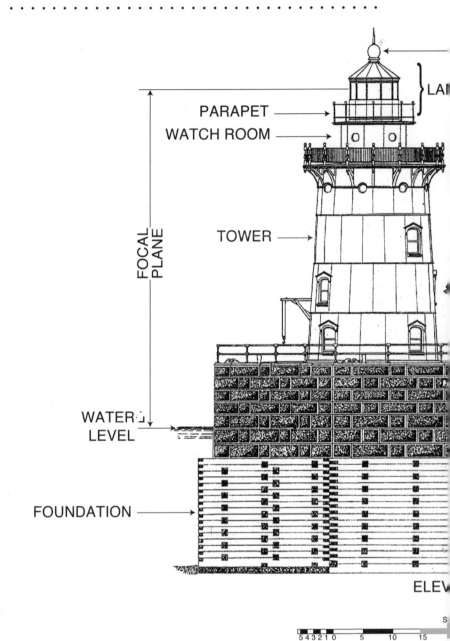

LA[...]

PARAPET

WATCH ROOM

FOCAL PLANE

TOWER

WATER LEVEL

FOUNDATION

ELEV[...]

5 4 3 2 1 0   5   10   15

DETROIT RIV[...]

6

VENTILATOR BALL

ERN ROOM

GLOSSARY OF TERMS

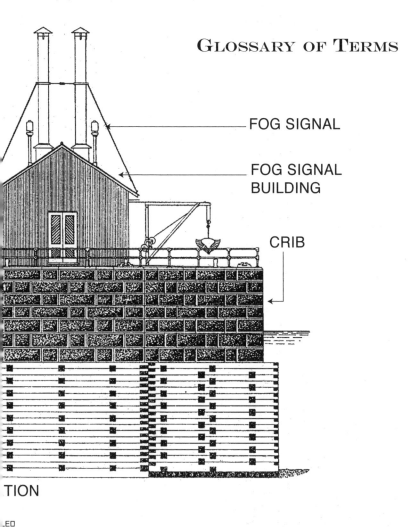

FOG SIGNAL

FOG SIGNAL
BUILDING

CRIB

TION

ED

| 25 | 30 | 35 | 40 | 45 feet |

LIGHTHOUSE

SOME THINGS ABOUT
LIGHTHOUSES

Optics used in lighthouses can be confusing to the new light buff. Fortunately, the optics that were originally installed in most Great Lakes lights are only three of the six types or "Orders" of lens. Augustin Fresnel, a French Physicist, developed a type of hand-ground crystal lens that could both refract and reflect the light from a modest source and beam it across great distances. The lens types were named for Fresnel, pronounced "Fra-nel," and he categorized them into six "Orders." The higher the Order of the lens, the shorter the range. Most of the lighthouses on the Great Lakes were equipped with Third Order Fresnels. Many were equipped with Fourth Order Fresnel lens, and a very few were equipped with Second Order Fresnels.

Fuels for the lights ranged from whale oil to kerosene to electricity. Acetylene and even natural gas were used to illuminate the beacons. The biggest innovation came when electricity became reliable as a power-source to be used at the lights. With electric power came automation. An unending and reliable source of power meant that keepers were no longer required to watch over the

Conical

Skeletal

Pyramidal

Pyramidal Style   Schoolhouse   Square/integral

lights, and that job soon became obsolete. With the absence of lightkeepers, however, came the thieves and vandals. Soon many historic lights fell into disrepair and outright destruction.

On the lakes, the introduction of radar on lakeboats made them largely independent of many of the lighthouses. Additionally the shifting of navigation routes caused by the shifting in demand for assorted lake products changed the need for some of the lights

Round

in some places. Today, few lighthouses are really needed in the navigation of lakeboats and many of the sites have taken on new roles as museums or private residences.

When speaking about lighthouses, there are many terms that are commonly used, and by becoming familiar with these terms, the reader can better understand this book. Pictured on these pages are seven common structures of the Great Lakes.

THE HEART OF THE GREAT LAKES

here have been four products that have been at the heart of Great
Lakes navigation. Lumber, iron ore, coal and grain have always
been the major cargoes carried on the lakes. These cargoes have
evolved in their importance over the passing of history. Grain was the first true
bulk product to be transported across the lakes. Granted, the fur trade had been
popular in the earliest decades of lake commerce, but this product was one of
wilderness production and by the late 1820s, grain had become the favored
product to be carried aboard lakeboats. To this day, the rich grain harvests of the
western states are still a primary bulk commodity. In the early days of lake transportation, grain vessels started in Chicago and hauled their cargoes east to the

10

ports of Buffalo and Oswego. There the product was unloaded by hand and shovel and carried ashore on the backs of immigrants, one bushel basket at a time. In 1841 a man named Joseph Dart invented a contraption that would reach down and extend a series of buckets on a belt into the hold of a grain-laden vessel and scoop up the cargo. The contraption was a wild success and soon "Dart's Legs" were extended from every grain elevator on the lakes, and thousands of immigrants were unemployed. The movement of grain was increased by ten fold, and lakes commerce boomed.

Iron ore was discovered on the upper lakes nearly as soon as Europeans began exploring the region. The ore lay right at the surface and it is said that all one needed to do was stick the toe of his boot into the soil and ore could be claimed. The problem was that there was little use for such red-dirt in the early 1800s. All of that changed rapidly as the science of steel production was developed and the massive steel plants began to grow on the lower lakes. Soon there was a new place for those immigrants to find work, and those steel mills grew hungry for iron ore. When the locks at Sault Saint Marie opened in 1854, the way was cleared for the ore ranges of the Lake Superior region to feed the steel mills of the lower lakes. Soon the flow of ore grew into the life-blood of the Great Lakes maritime industry, and remains as such to this day. Another of the natural resources that was harvested and transported across the lakes was lumber. When exploration of the region began, the area was one dense forest all of the way from Lake Ontario to Lake Superior. As luck would have it, most of the creations of civilization were made primarily of wood, and thus lumber became the product in the greatest demand across the lakes. By the end of the 1880s, lumber was rapidly being replaced as the top bulk cargo by iron ore, and by World War I, the lumber industry was in a rapid decline. The factors that lead to the fall of king lumber were the decline in the use of lumber in construction and the decline in suitable trees to be harvested within the region. The on-set of the "Great Depression" of the 1930s completely killed the transportation of lumber on the Great Lakes.

As a bulk cargo, coal just seemed to slip onto the scene. At first the cargoes of coal were shipped west from Buffalo and Sandusky as ballast in the holds of west-bound grain vessels. Most places that required fuel for heat or steam simply used wood, which was much more available and far less expensive than coal. Even lakeboats that were steam powered used wood as their fuel. Soon, however, it became clear that wood was far less efficient as a fuel than was coal. An early steamer would have to be loaded with 25 to 30 cords of wood and would consume all of that within 36 to 40 hours. This fuel would take up most of the boat's deck space and had to be both loaded and fed to the boilers by hand. A few yards of coal, however could do the same work, take up far less space and could be dumped aboard and shoveled from a hoppered bunker. By 1857, coal had become the major fuel of the Great Lakes steamers, and was rapidly becoming the primary fuel source of the region. For the next century, coal powered most of the lakeboats and was also a profitable cargo. Today, coal remains one of the primary cargoes of the lakes.

Other cargoes such as stone, potash and petroleum products are also carried across the Great Lakes, and with the movement of these many products, there was a need for navigation aids. The need for lights to mark the dangers has never ended, but the use of modern navigation equipment has dramatically decreased the need. Through the use of the Global Positioning System's satellites, anyone with a hand-held GPS receiver that costs only a few hundred dollars, can pinpoint their exact position to within a few feet at any place on the Great Lakes. To be blunt, there is no longer any practical need for lighthouses as aids to navigation. Their use now is best seen in the role of historic places. For that reason alone, every lighthouse must be preserved.

THE
LIGHTS
OF LAKE
ONTARIO

GREAT LAKES LIGHTHOUSES

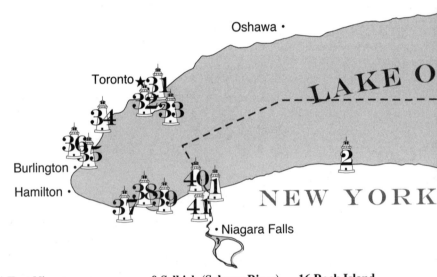

ONTARIO

Oshawa •

LAKE O

Toronto ★31
32 33
34

36 5
5

Burlington •

Hamilton •

2

40
41
38 39
37

NEW YORK

• Niagara Falls

1 Fort Niagara	9 Selkirk (Salmon River)	16 Rock Island
2 Thirty Mile Point	10 Stony Point	17 Sunken Rock
3 Braddock Point	11 Galloo Island	18 Sisters Island
4 Charlotte-Genesee	12 Sacket's Harbor	19 Crossover Island
5 Rochester Harbor	(Horse Island)	20 Ogdensburg Harbor
6 Old Sodus Point	13 Tibbetts Point	21 Windmill Point
7 Sodus Outer	14 Cape Vincent	22 Prescott Breakwater
8 Oswego West Pierhead	Breakwater	23 Prescott Visitors'
	15 East Charity Shoal	Center

14

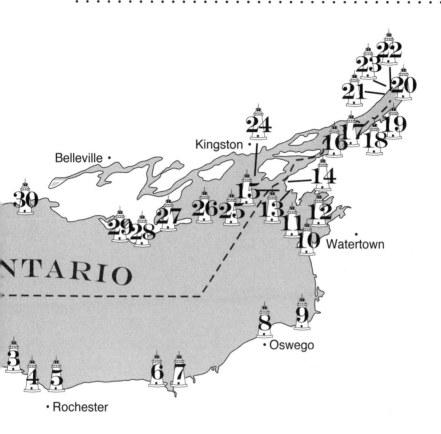

Belleville •

Kingston •

Watertown •

ONTARIO

• Oswego

• Rochester

Lake Ontario

It is commonly held that Lake Ontario was discovered by Etienne Brul'e in 1615. This would be surprising to members of the Iroquois who were residing along the lake's shore for many centuries before lace-garbed French explorers came stumbling upon the area. Being the smallest of the five freshwater seas, this eldest duchess in the royal lineage of the Great Lakes also happens to be one of the deepest of the group. A deep sounding of 127 fathoms, or 762 feet, can be found on the Lake Ontario chart. This measurement is greater than the greatest depth on Lake Huron or Erie and comparable to Lake Michigan's maximum depth. Lake Superior, of course, stands as queen of the inland seas being the deepest and coldest of all.

From the French and Indian War to the Revolutionary War to the War of 1812 and the Civil War, Lake Ontario has had action on its surface by the combatants. At this moment, the remains of vessels sent to the bottom over that span of events rest preserved on Lake Ontario's bottom as if stored in an ice water museum. There is even a rumor that a German U-boat took a shot at a freighter on Lake Ontario during World War II. The Canadian Coast Guard promptly went out and responded by bombing a shoal that appeared to be shaped like a submarine, but no one has ever confirmed the presence of "das unterseeboot." The story smacks more of legend than of fact, and was probably just a case of war nerves. Lake Ontario has seen plenty of that.

Along with the early settlement of the Lake Ontario region came some of the earliest navigation and navigation aids. As a result some of the earliest lighthouses on the lakes are located in this region. The first true "lighthouse" on the Great Lakes was constructed in 1804 at Fort George (then Fort Mississauga) to aid navigation around the mouth of the Niagara River. This same light was removed in the year 1814, at the end of the War of 1812. The first light that was intended to aid Great Lakes navigation, however, was established in one of the lookout towers at Fort Niagara in 1781 and a light was maintained at that site until 1993.

Commerce on Lake Ontario continued at a steady pace until the onset of the "Great Depression" of the 1930s. Unfortunately, after World War II, the commerce that took seed on the other lakes boomed and swiftly overshadowed Lake Ontario. Still, the Lake Ontario region is one which is rich in history and heritage as is its lighthouses.

1 Fort Niagara

☐ Visited on

_____

Established: (1781, 1823) 1872*
Status: Inactive; museum
Location: (NY) On riverbank just south of Old Fort Niagara
Type: Octagonal
Access: Car
About the Light: *Current structure from 1872 was active until May 13, 1993. The service building houses a museum and gift shop. Take Route 18F or the Robert Moses Parkway into Fort Niagara State Park then follow the signs. The first Lighthouse established at Niagara was a lantern placed on the roof of Fort Niagara's "French Castle" by the British in 1781. A second tower called the Newark Light was built by the British at Fort Mississauga on the Canadian bank of the river and stood from 1804 to 1814. The current tower is the fourth to serve the area.*

2 Thirty Mile Point

☐ Visited on

_____

Established: 1875
Status: Inactive; museum
Location: (NY) In the Golden Hill State Park, 12 miles east of Olcott
Type: Square/integral
Access: Car
About the Light: *Deactivated in 1958 when the light was moved to an automated steel tower nearby, the historic light is located safely within the protection of the state park, this rough brick structure is secure from vandals and contains a museum. The site can be reached by following New York Route 18 to Carmen Road and following it to the state park. Camping is allowed in this park and the view of Lake Ontario is second to none.*

3 Braddock Point

☐ Visited on

_____

Established: 1896
Status: Inactive; private residence
Location: (NY) Just west of Braddock Bay, 20 miles northwest of Rochester
Type: Octagonal
Access: Car, may be viewed from public road
About the Light: *The tower and dwelling were a near duplicate of the Cleveland (Ohio) light of 1829 which was torn down in 1895, and whose lantern, lens and metalwork were used to complete the Braddock light. Deactivated in 1954, the original 110 foot tower was cut down by two-thirds by the Coast Guard due to extensive structural damage. The partial wooden reconstruction was completed by the owners in 1996. Find the lighthouse near the end of Lighthouse Road off Lake Ontario State Parkway.*

*Throughout, dates in parentheses denote earlier structures at or near the same site.

4 Charlotte-Genesee ☐ Visited on

Established: 1822
_____

Status: Inactive; museum
Location: (NY) Genesee River near Rochester
Type: Conical/octagonal
Access: Car
About the Light: *One of the oldest light structures on the Great Lakes, it was deactivated in 1881 and was decapitated in 1884 when its lantern room and*
lens were removed to a "new" wooden structure on the west pier. The current lantern room is a wooden reconstruction installed in 1984, one hundred years later, along with a Fourth Order Fresnel lens that was the original from the lighthouse at Lorain, Ohio. Drive west out of Rochester and take Lake Avenue north toward Ontario Beach Park. The light will be found just before entering the park.

5 Rochester Harbor ☐ Visited on

Established: (1822, 1931) 1995
_____

Status: Active
Location: (NY) North end of the west pier
Type: Modern steel cylinder
Access: Foot
About the Light: *The west pier light has been moved and improved many times over the years as the pier has been lengthened and upgraded.*
Marking the entrance to the Genesee River and the Port of Rochester, it supplanted the old lighthouse on the hill (1822) in 1881 and has continued to do so ever since. To reach the west pier, continue north on Lake Avenue to Ontario Beach Park and walk from there.

6 Old Sodus Point ☐ Visited on

Established: (1825) 1871
_____

Status: Inactive; museum
Location: (NY) Lake-front, at the foot of Ontario Street, west of Sodus Bay.
Type: Square/integral
Access: Car
About the Light: *This structure replaced the original stone tower of 1825. Construction began in 1870, but the lighthouse officially went into service in 1871. Also during 1870, a perma-*
nent beacon (Sodus Outer) was installed at the end of the west pier marking the entrance to Sodus Bay. In 1901, the Lighthouse Board determined that the pier light was suffi-cient and deactivated the shore light, although the keeper's house remained in use by the Coast Guard until 1984.

7 Sodus Outer

☐ Visited on

_____

Established: (1834, 1858, 1870) 1901
Status: Active
Location: (NY) On the end of the Sodus Bay west pier
Type: Square
Access: Car
About the Light: *The current structure dates from 1901. By 1834, the first piers were constructed at the entrance to Sodus Bay and a beacon placed at the end. A permanent beacon was installed in 1870. By 1901, the new light alone was deemed sufficient for the traffic in the area and the shore light was deactivated. From the Old Sodus Lighthouse, continue east along the lakefront, then north once the west shore of the bay has been reached to a small park at the base of the west pier.*

8 Oswego West Pierhead ☐ Visited on

_____

Established: (1836) 1934
Status: Active
Location: (NY) On the end of the west breakwater at the entrance to the port of Oswego
Type: Square/integral steel tower
Access: Boat, but can be seen by driving to the river mouth
About the Light: *There have been three lighthouses at Oswego. The present structure was erected in 1934 at the end of a new stone west pier. It replaced the old west pier light of 1836-1930. The lighthouse was the site of a tragedy in December 1942 when six Coast Guardsmen were killed in a boating accident while changing keepers. Since then, the light has earned the reputation of being haunted. To the relief of many, it was automated in 1968. Best viewed from Breitbeck Park.*

9 Selkirk (Salmon River) ☐ Visited on

_____

Established: 1838
Status: Private residence
Location: (NY) On the north side mouth of the Salmon River
Type: Octagonal
Access: Car
About the Light: *This is the only completely intact example of an original "bird-cage" style lantern room left on the Great Lakes. "Bird-cage" lantern rooms pre-date the change over to Fresnel lenses from the old system of Argand lamps and reflectors. Had the lighthouse not been decommissioned at an early date (1858) the lantern room would have undergone rebuilding to accommodate a new lens. To reach the light, take NY Route 3 to the town of Port Ontario and turn east on County Road 5 to its end.*

10 Stony Point

☐ Visited on

Established: (1830) 1869
Status: Inactive, private residence
Location: (NY) On the end of Stony Point, six miles east of the town of Henderson Harbor.
Type: Square/integral, brick tower and dwelling
Access: Car
About the Light: *This light is very similar in design to the Horse Island light. Erected in 1869, it replaced a previous 1830 lighthouse at the same site. It was deactivated in 1945. Please view this light from the public road. From NY Route 3, take Military Road on the south side of Henderson Harbor to Lighthouse Road (County Road 178) to its end.*

11 Galloo Island

☐ Visited on

Established: (1820) 1867
Status: Active; light and island privately owned
Location: (NY) Southwest end of Galloo Island, six miles into Lake Ontario
Type: Conical limestone tower with attached dwelling
Access: Boat
About the Light: *The present lighthouse was erected in 1867. All that is in working order on this site is the light, which is automated. The stone-block tower is worn by the lake and the keeper's quarters and other nearby structures are boarded up. Its location on a remote islands in Lake Ontario is all that is sparing this site the damage done by vandals.*

12 Sacket's Harbor (Horse Island)

☐ Visited on

Established: (1831) 1870
Status: Inactive; light and island privately owned
Location: (NY) Horse Island at the entrance to Sacket's Harbor
Type: Square/integral brick tower and dwelling
Access: Boat
About the Light: *Very similar in design to the Stony Point light, it is stuck in the corner of Lake Ontario. This light and its adjacent keeper's quarters are easily overlooked today. In the former days of Lake Ontario navigation, however, Sacket's Harbor was a busy place and this light played great favor to many a mariner. When the leaves are off the tress, it is visible from the adjacent Sacket's Harbor Battlefield.*

13 Tibbetts Point

☐ Visited on

Established: (1827) 1854
Status: Active
Location: (NY) 2-1/2 miles west of Cape Vincent on Lighthouse Road
Type: Conical brick tower covered in stucco
Access: Car
About the Light: *Tibbets Point marks the entrance into the St. Lawrence River. The tower was built in 1854 to replace the original rubble-stone tower of 1827. A Coast Guard station until May, 1981, the keeper's dwelling now serves as an American Youth Hostel. The Tibbetts Point Lighthouse Society was formed in 1988 for the purpose of preserving the lighthouse and its grounds as an educational and historic entity.*

14 Cape Vincent Breakwater

☐ Visited on

Established: 1900
Status: Inactive, displaced
Location: (NY) Southern approach to Cape Vincent on Route 12E
Type: Short square wooden tower, now aluminum-sided
Access: Car
About the Light: *One of two such lights originally erected at each end of the village breakwall, this light was deactivated in 1934 and subsequently moved from its location, as an aid to navigation, to a place near the town office complex in 1951. Driving down Route 12E, the sharp-eyed lighthouse buff can spot the remains of the lighthouse squatting near the office complex. It is open to the public.*

15 East Charity Shoal

☐ Visited on

Established: 1935
Status: Active
Location: (NY) Six miles southwest of the entrance of the St. Lawrence River
Type: Octagonal cast iron tower
Access: Boat
About the Light: *The 30-foot light tower rests on a 10-foot high octagonal concrete pedestal, and both sit on a square concrete crib that is 12 feet high itself. This light first went into service in 1877 in Vermilion, Ohio, but was removed in 1929 after a severe ice storm nearly toppled it. Transported to Buffalo, modifications were made and the tower was later re-erected at its present site. The disposition of their missing lighthouse perplexed Vermilion residents for 65 years until 1994 when the mystery was accidentally solved.*

16 Rock Island

☐ Visited on

_____

Established: (1847) 1882
Status: Inactive
Location: (NY) 4 miles northeast of Clayton on St. Lawrence River
Type: Conical, cast iron
Access: Boat
About the Light: *Constructed in 1882, this light replaced the combination lighthouse/keeper's house of 1847. Deactivated in 1958, the State of New York maintains it as a park in their Thousand Island region. The tower is open to the public when manned. From the U.S. mainland, the island is visible from the hamlet of Fishers Landing off Route 12 at Route 180, just a few miles southwest of the Thousand Island Bridge.*

17 Sunken Rock

☐ Visited on

_____

Established: (1847) 1882
Status: Active
Location: (NY) Just east of Alexandria Bay
Type: Conical cast iron
Access: Boat
About the Light: *Just two stories tall, the tiny tower matches the nearly-invisible island on which it has been constructed. This area, however, is one where the waters of the St. Lawrence are very swift and currents are strong. Giant lakeboats and salt-water visitors to the lakes glide by so close that they seem to touch the rock itself.*

18 Sisters Island

☐ Visited on

_____

Established: 1870
Status: Inactive; private residence
Location: (NY) 12 miles NE of Alexandria Bay
Type: Square/integral limestone tower
Access: Boat
About the Light: *Showing much of the "stick" architecture that was so popular in the 1870s, the keeper's quarters is constructed with the three-story tower as an extension of the building. As a part of the Thousand Islands chain, the island on which the light stands seems just big enough to support the structure. The walls of the light tower and keeper's quarters are made of cut stone and add greatly to the appeal of the lighthouse.*

19 Crossover Island

☐ Visited on

_____

Established: (1848) 1882
Status: Inactive; privately owned
Location: (NY) 4 miles NE of Chippewa Bay
Type: Conical, cast iron
Access: Boat
About the Light: *Crossover Island takes its name from the fact that this was where ships crossed from the U.S. to the Canadian side of the channel. Completely rebuilt in 1882, it replaced the original 1848 light that consisted of a dwelling with the tower attached. The light is visible from the scenic overlook on Route 12 east of Chippewa Bay.*

20 Ogdensburg Harbor

☐ Visited on

_____

Established: (1834) 1900
Status: Inactive; private residence
Location: (NY) On the tip of Lighthouse Point which makes up the mouth of the Oswegatchie River.
Type: Square/integral limestone tower and dwelling
Access: Boat; private property, not visible from road
About the Light: *Very similar in design to the lights at Stony Point and Horse Island, this light stands 65 feet high. It was built on the site of an old fort which was used to fend off local Indians by the French as they gained a foothold in the area. Later, the site was also used for a "pest house" for cholera victims.*

21 Windmill Point

☐ Visited on

_____

Established: 1873
Status: Inactive
Location: (ONT) On St. Lawrence River 1.3 miles east of Prescott on Hwy 2 (King Street)
Type: Conical stone tower
Access: Car
About the Light: *Originally built as a windmill in the 1920s, the tower was converted into a lighthouse in 1873 and deactivated in 1978. In 1838, the Battle of the Windmill took place here. During the Patriot War, a group of Americans and Canadian rebels launched an attack from Ogdensburg hoping to wrest control of nearby Fort Wellington from the British. The Americans took refuge in the windmill, from which they defied the besiegers for several days until guns brought down from Kingston forced their surrender.*

22 Prescott Breakwater

☐ Visited on
_____

Established:
Status: Active
Location: (ONT) End of rocky pier separating city marina from
St. Lawrence River
Type: Short octagonal wooden tower
Access: Boat
About the Light: *Also known as Prescott Harbor Outer Light,
this 20-foot tower rises to support a bright green lantern and
parapet and functions as an entry light for the city marina.*

23 Prescott Visitors' Center

☐ Visited on
_____

Established:
Status: Private aid to navigation
Location: (ONT) Overlooks Prescott city marina
Type: Octagonal wooden tower
Access: Car
About the Light: *This is a 40-foot-high modern replica with a
Fresnel lens donated by the Canadian Coast Guard.*

24 Nine Mile Point

☐ Visited on
_____

Established: 1833
Status: Inactive
Location: (ONT) On the southwest point of Simcoe Island
Type: Cylindrical, rough stone
Access: Carferry
About the Light: *Nine Mile Point light was a landfall light for
vessels making for the St. Lawrence from Lake Ontario. At 45
feet in height, this light was identical to the 1833 light built at
Pointe Petre, which was 17 feet taller. Taking a carferry from
Kingston to Wolfe Island, then another to Simcoe Island, will provide access to the light.*

25 Main Duck Island

☐ Visited on

Established: 1914
Status: Active
Location: (ONT) Northern end of Main Duck Island
Type: Octagonal reinforced concrete
Access: Boat
About the Light: *This light marks one of the busiest areas of traffic in and out of the St. Lawrence Seaway. The tower stretches more than 74 feet tall and has vacant keeper's quarters nearby.* SEE STORY BEGINNING ON PAGE 33.

26 Old False Duck Island

☐ Visited on

Established: 1828
Status: Inactive; museum
Location: (ONT) Mariners' Memorial Park and Museum, South Bay, Prince Edward County in eastern Quinte Island
Type: Cylindrical stone tower
Access: Car
About the Light: *Only the lantern room, lens and parapet are original, removed from the 63-foot tower when it was deactivated in 1965 and placed on this reproduction 30 foot tower in 1967. The entire assembly is a part of the mariners' park and outstanding exhibits that exist there. Getting to the site is a bit of a trek. Either CR-17 or CR-18 will lead to the winding country road that is CR-9. Near the intersection of CR-9 and CR-13 the lighthouse and mariners' park can be found.*

27 Prince Edward Point ☐ Visited on

Established: 1881
Status: Inactive
Location: (ONT) On the southeast end of Quinte Island
Type: Pyramidal wooden tower and dwelling
Access: Car
About the Light: *Deactivated in 1959, the lantern room was removed when the modern steel-framed tower that is still in use went into service the same year. From 1881 to 1941, the old 36-foot-high tower displayed a fixed red light, giving it the name "Red Onion." In 1941, the red light was changed to green. Locals refer to this light as the "Point Traverse Lighthouse" even though, technically, it is situated on Prince Edward Point. After visiting the False Duck Island light, follow CR-9 south the the end.*

28 Pointe Petre

☐ Visited on
_____

Established: (1833) 1967
Status: Active
Location: (ONT) Southwest tip of Quinte Island
Type: Cylindrical reinforced concrete
Access: Car
About the Light: *Pointe Petre remains an active Government Environment Research installation, so access is restricted. The modern tower stands 60 feet tall. The original masonry tower, at 62 feet in height, was identical to the 1833 light built at Nine Mile Point, which was 17 feet shorter. Structural weakness forced its demolition. Pointe Petre is about 12 miles from the town of Picton. Take CR-10 to its end. A good look can be had from the gate.*

29 Salmon Point (Wicked Point)

☐ Visited on
_____

Established: 1871
Status: Inactive; private residence
Location: (ONT) On the southwestern tip of Quinte Island
Type: Pyramidal wooden tower and attached dwelling
Access: Car
About the Light: *In Lake Ontario's heyday of maritime traffic, this light marked a dangerous area of reefs and shoals. By 1917, however, the traffic in this part of the lake was slimming and the light was deactivated. The wooden structure stands 40 feet tall and is currently part of a privately-operated campground. From Picton, Ontario follow CR-10 until it branches off into CR-18 and follow that road to the end where the campgrounds and lighthouse can be found.*

30 Presqu'ile Point

☐ Visited on
_____

Established: 1840
Status: Active
Location: (ONT) On the east end of the point, directly below the city of Brighton
Type: Octagonal stone tower sheathed in wooden shingles
Access: Car
About the Light: *Located within the Presqu'ile Provincial Park, the 67 foot tower now has a modern plastic optic on top. The original lantern room has been removed. To access the site, follow the signs from the city of Brighton to the Provincial Park.*

31 Toronto Harbour Aquatic Park

☐ Visited on
_____

Established: 1974
Status: Active
Location: (ONT) Southern most tip of Tommy Thompson Park
Type: Octagonal welded steel
Access: Car/then long walk on foot
About the Light: *Tommy Thompson Park is located at the foot of Leslie Street (turn south off Lakeshore Blvd.) on the Toronto waterfront. The park is open to the public year 'round on week-ends and holidays except Christmas, Boxing Day and New Years Day. The peninsula that comprises the park was constructed on landfill starting back in the late 1950s and was originally intended to serve as an outer harbor to accommodate an expected increase in shipping associated with the opening of the St. Lawrence Seaway in 1959.*

32 Gibraltar Point

☐ Visited on
_____

Established: 1808
Status: Inactive (an adjacent modern steel skeleton tower is active)
Location: (ONT) Southwest end of Centre Island
Type: Hexagonal limestone tower
Access: Passenger ferry/then foot
About the Light: *This lighthouse is the oldest in existence on the Great Lakes. Originally built to a height of 67 feet, a 15-foot extension was added in 1932. The first keeper of the light died suddenly under mysterious circumstances; the subsequent discovery of a human skele-ton nearby gave rise to the legend that the lighthouse was haunted. Deactivated in 1958, the site is lovingly maintained by the Metro Toronto Parks Board. From the foot of Yonge Street, take the ferry to Hanlan's Point.*

33 Queen's Wharf

☐ Visited on
_____

Established: (1838) 1855
Status: Inactive; display
Location: (ONT) Within a street car loop at the intersection of Fleet Street and Lakeshore Blvd.
Type: Short square wooden tower (less than 20 feet overall)
Access: Car
About the Light: *Originally located on the end of a wharf at the present intersection of Fleet and Bathhurst Streets, the light-house was moved to its present site in 1929 when that part of Toronto Harbour was filled in as part of a large-scale land reclamation plan. It now lies almost half a mile from the water and is well maintained.*

34 Oakville

☐ Visited on

_____

Established: (1837) 1889
Status: Inactive
Location: (ONT) South of the Lakeshore Bridge (Hwy 2) and east of Forsythe Street at marina
Type: Tapering hexagonal wooden tower
Access: Car
About the Light: *This 1889 structure replaced the original 1837 light when it was destroyed by a fierce storm in April 1886. In the early 1960s, the light was removed from service and placed on display at a private marina on 16 Mile Creek, but polite visitors can access the light. Taking Lakeshore Road (Hwy 2) through Oakville and turning towards the lake at Forsythe Street will lead to the marina.*

35 Burlington Canal Front Range

☐ Visited on

_____

Established: (1842, 1856, 1909) Modern
Status: Active
Location: (ONT) East end of Burlington Canal south pier
Type: Reinforced concrete
Access: Car/then foot
About the Light: *Burlington Canal, which connects Burlington Bay to Lake Ontario, was first opened in 1832. The canal and its piers have been modified many times over the years, as were the lights at the end of the south pier. Old Burlington Main Light (below) was the rear light of the range. See directions below.*

36 Burlington Main

☐ Visited on

_____

Established: (1837) 1858
Status: Inactive
Location: (ONT) South side of the Burlington Canal
Type: Cylindrical limestone tower
Access: Car
About the Light: *This "fire-proof" limestone tower was built to replace the original wood lighthouse of 1837 that was destroyed in a pier fire in 1856 set off by the sparks of a passing steamer. Standing 55 feet tall, the structure is in bad condition as it was deactivated in 1961 and has not been well tended. Also in bad shape nearby is the brick keeper's house. From Highway 2 to the north or from Queen Elizabeth Way to the south, take Beach Blvd. to East Port Drive which passes by the light.*

37 Port Dalhousie Front Range

☐ Visited on

_____

Established: 1879
Status: Active
Location: (ONT) North end of 1500-foot-long east pier at Port Dalhousie Harbour
Type: Pyramidal wooden tower, now aluminum sided
Access: Car/then foot
About the Light: *From 1829 to 1932, Port Dalhousie was the northern terminus of the first three Welland Canals, connecting Lakes Ontario and Erie. These range lights helped guide ships into the canal. Both lights were automated in 1968, and the rear light was deactivated in 1988. The rear light of 1898 replaced the lights of 1852 (destroyed by fire) and 1893 (destroyed by lightning). Both lights are now part of a very nice beach and marina complex. From Lakeshore Road, turn north onto Lighthouse Road; follow it to the marina.*

38 Port Dalhousie Rear Range

☐ Visited on

_____

Established: (1852, 2893) 1898
Status: Inactive
Location: (ONT) Near shore end of 1500-foot-long east pier at Port Dalhousie Harbour
Type: Octagonal wooden tower, now aluminum sided
Access: Car
About the Light: *From 1829 to 1932, Port Dalhousie was the northern terminus of the first three Welland Canals, connecting Lakes Ontario and Erie. These range lights helped guide ships into the canal. Both lights were automated in 1968, and the rear light was deactivated in 1988. The rear light of 1898 replaced the lights of 1852 (destroyed by fire) and 1893 (destroyed by lightning). Both lights are now part of a very nice beach and marina complex. From Lakeshore Road, turn north onto Lighthouse Road; follow it to the marina.*

39 Port Weller Outer

☐ Visited on

_____

Established: 1931
Status: Active
Location: (ONT) North end of Port Weller west pier
Type: "Arts Decoratifs," or art deco; reinforced concrete
Access: Boat
About the Light: *This light is right out of a 1930s movie. The cement foundation is stylishly molded in the "Arts Decoratifs," or art deco, fashion of that era. This light continues to guide ships into the man-made harbor of Port Weller, which became the fourth and current northern terminus of the Welland Canal in 1932. An active Coast Guard Base at the northern end of Government Road prohibits access by car. The best view is by boat or from across the canal at the north end of the east pier, which is accessible by car.*

40 Niagara River Front Range

☐ Visited on

_____

Established: 1903
Status: Active
Location: (ONT) Town of Niagara-on-the-Lake; west bank of river mouth
Type: Pyramidal wooden tower
Access: Car
About the Light: *The Niagara River Range Lights mark the entrance to the mouth of the river. The front range light sits within a privately-operated marina, but polite visitors may gain access via the parking lot. From Ricardo Street in town, turn east onto Melville Street to the Marina entrance. The rear range light may be seen a short distance away down river.*

41 Niagara River Rear Range

☐ Visited on

_____

Established: 1903
Status: Active
Location: (ONT) Town of Niagara-on-the-Lake; west bank of river mouth
Type: Pyramidal wooden tower
Access: Car
About the Light: *The Niagara River Range Lights mark the entrance to the mouth of the river. The rear range light sits next to a private residence at the foot of Collingwood Street. Turn east onto Collingwood from Ricardo Street (see above). The front range light may be seen a short distance away up river near the marina fuel dock.*

EIGHT FRUSTRATING DAYS

Today, giant "maximum size" freighters snail across the surface of Lake Ontario hauling huge cargoes and earning big money. As each type of modern vessel passes Main Duck Island and its big lighthouse in the far eastern end of the lake on their way to and from the Saint Lawrence Seaway, the goal is the same: *do not delay and make every second work toward a profit.* Whether the vessel is Canadian or American, or a saltwater visitor to the lakes, the urgency remains unchanged. One of these big steel vessels can cost more than $1,000 per hour to operate, and so the boats are often equipped with self-unloading booms to cut the time needed to discharge their loads. Bow thrusters, state-of-the-art radar and other electronic navigation tools are standard equipment, all intended to push the boundary of efficiency and increase the speeds, thus maximizing the profits. Therein is found the formula of the vessel owners and management: *capacity, speed, and the best of equipment equals maximum profit.* In 1920, however, Captain Harry Randall had a very different philosophy of earning a profit for the boat that he owned and ran across Lake Ontario.

For Captain Randall, the key to making a tidy profit was in the running of a tiny steamer, staffing the boat with the minimum crew, and making as many cargo runs as he could between break up of the spring ice and the next winter's freeze. It was not that the good captain was cheap, or careless. Rather this was the way that the maritime Randall klan had always conducted their family business, which was the operation of the tiny steamer JOHN RANDALL. Constructed in 1905, the RANDALL's schooner-type hull was just 116 feet long and 22 feet wide. Propelled by a modest steam engine, the little boat kept the Randall family employed by busily shuttling small cargoes of bulk freight between the Canadian and U.S. ports on the eastern-most end of Lake Ontario. She was a small, economical and handy vessel that was well-suited to maneuvering through the inlets, bays and islands of the Canadian coast. By 1920 the

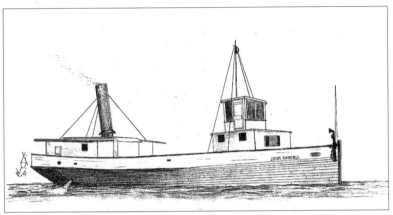

The little steamer JOHN RANDALL stranded on Main Duck Island in a mid-November storm of 1920. Her crew would surely have perished had it not been for the kindness of the local lighthouse keeper.

– Author's Drawing

little steamer had been handed down through the family and was now under the command of 29-year-old Captain Harry Randall, the son of the vessel's namesake. As the navigation season of that year passed, Captain Randall had maintained the family's hard-working tradition and kept the family steamer busy.

As the navigation season on Lake Ontario grew late, the autumn gales began to sweep the area. This meant Captain Randall had to time his trips across the lake so that each passage came between the storms. In an era when weather forecasting was in its infancy, this timing was guess-work at best. Often when the little steamer was on the open lake the weather would suddenly become enraged and Captain Randall would be forced to run for cover behind one of the many islands in the eastern lake. To add to the woes of operating the diminutive lakeboat was the economics of its staffing. Using a crew of only five men, Captain Randall was operating a steamer that was vastly understaffed. Every member of the vessel's crew had to pull triple duty just to get through any one trip. Add on the hours spent at anchor in shelter from a storm, and you have a great potential for trouble.

On Tuesday, November 16th, 1920, Captain Harry Randall ordered the lines of the JOHN RANDALL cast off from the D.L.&W. coal trestle at Oswego, New York. A cargo of 250 tons of coal aboard the family steamer was consigned to R. Downey & Company of Belleville, Ontario. It was an ordinary cargo and an ordinary trip that would have extraordinary consequences and a foreshadowing of a disaster to come for Captain Randall. Lake Ontario appeared tranquil as the JOHN RANDALL left the protection of the harbor and headed north toward Prince Edward Bay. The journey would require a 52-mile dash north to the Canadian coast and the inlet of Adolphus Reach. From there the boat would have to zigzag some 35 miles west along "The Narrows" to the town of Belleville. Guessing that the RANDALL made an average speed of about eight miles per hour, the trip up should have taken about 12 hours in good weather.

Once out in the expanse of Lake Ontario, the evening turned to night around the JOHN RANDALL. With that same November night came the beginnings of a furious gale. The winds boomed across the surface of the lake and the waves tossed the little lakeboat like a toy. Soon the seas were coming aboard the boat and the water found her hatches. Being just slightly larger than a tug, the RANDALL had not been designed to take this kind of weather, and in short order she was taking aboard large quantities of Lake Ontario. It soon became clear that the boat was certain to sink, and Captain Randall decided to seek shelter and pump out his vessel. Off to the port side the lighthouse of Main Duck Island became visible and Captain Randall directed his boat toward it. He had sailed past the island hundreds of times and often sheltered there, so the area was a very familiar shore. Instinctively, Captain Randall headed for the inlet called School House Bay on the island. If he could get his boat into the shelter of the bay, he would be shielded from the waves and wind and he could cheat the lake from taking away his command. It was just after midnight on Wednesday, and the entire exhausted crew of the JOHN RANDALL was in a life-and-death struggle with Lake Ontario.

Wednesday passed and the little steamer did not appear at the Belleville dock. At that point there was little concern in maritime circles over the fate of the RANDALL. Captain Randall had often sheltered to wait out storms and a tardy arrival of his boat would not be unusual; it would be normal. Additionally, the storm continued to howl, and as long as the gale persisted, the RANDALL could be expected to shelter. Even as Thursday turned into Friday, the levels of concern did not go beyond the expected, but by the time that the weekend lapsed into the next week and the RANDALL remained absent, an atmosphere of great concern prevailed across the lake. Granted, the stormy conditions had persisted, but surely, Captain Randall would have found an opportunity to make a dash for some port, someplace. No harbor, however, reported any sign of the steamer. By Monday, the atmosphere on the eastern lake had gone from near panic to the resignation that the RANDALL had been taken by the lake. Vessels were asked to watch for signs of the wreck, and any bodies that may have been left on the surface.

On Tuesday, the 23rd of November, the hope that the boat and her crew had survived the lake's tantrum vanished. It had now been a full week since the tiny steamer had hauled her cargo of coal out of Oswego, and nothing had been heard of her or her people. It was certain that the lake had swallowed another boat and its crew and left behind not a crumb. Searches of the north shore, south shore, the inlets and Mexico Bay gave no results. It was certain now: the JOHN RANDALL would go down in Great Lakes lore as another boat that simply went away with all of her crew.

Sorrow over the fate of the RANDALL and her crew would have been somewhat tempered, had those on the mainland been able to speak to Fred Bougard. In that stormy November of 1920, Mr. Bougard was the keeper of the Main Duck Island lighthouse, and for the past week he had been keeping five house guests dry and warm at his lighthouse. Well fed and snugly comfortable were all five members of the steamer JOHN RANDALL. The problem was that the lake had been in such a tantrum for the preceding week that no one could get word off the island that the crew was safe and sound. It was not until Wednesday, exactly eight days after they had departed Oswego, that the crew were able to make their way to Picton, Ontario and tell their tale. Until then, they spent the time keeping the otherwise lonely lighthouse keeper company and sharing the lighthouse chores just to pass the time.

Often, Captain Randall had robbed Lake Ontario from her assault on his boat, and always the crafty master had recovered from the lake's beating and sailed on to his destination. This time, however, the lake had not been so easily outwitted. With the glow of the Main Duck Island in sight, the waves got the better of the steamer JOHN RANDALL. The flooding of the hold and compartments could not be stopped and the boat's pumps were completely overwhelmed. Within a mile of the safety of Main Duck Island, the RANDALL began to quickly founder. The lifeboats had long ago been washed over the side and there was only one escape for the crew: *they had to put on life-jackets and leap into the icewater.* Their only hope was to make the half-mile swim to the island in the frigid seas. The swim to the beach nearly proved deadly for the castaways, but they all made the beach. Benumbed, but alive, the five mariners began a hike to the north tip of the island where they knew that the warmth of the lighthouse awaited. Meanwhile, the lake pounded the remains of the steamer into wreckage.

When the wayward mariners reached the lighthouse, Keeper Bougard wrapped them in dry clothing and served up hot coffee. All of the near-frozen men were made comfortable until the keeper was sure that they were fully recovered. The downside was that, other than the callings of the lighthouse tender, Keeper Bougard had no way of communicating with anyone. Thus the ship-wrecked sailors were forced to wait out eight frustrating days while their next of kin considered them lost at sea.

There was great joy and relief at the end of the eight days of frustration, when it was announced that the crew of the RANDALL was safe. On Wednesday November 24th, the crew were back on home soil in Canada, and Captain Randall was going to have to start shopping for a new family lakeboat. The story, however, does not end there. Exactly one year later – to the day – Lake Ontario played its ultimate revenge on Captain Randall. Amid a furious gale, the lake took not only Captain Harry Randall, but also his new boat, the CITY OF NEW YORK. As if that were not enough, the lake also swallowed the captain's crew and along with them his wife and two children. The whole thrilling and tragic story is documented in this author's book, *Ghost Ships, Gales and Forgotten Tales.*

38

THE LIGHTS OF LAKE ERIE

GREAT LAKES LIGHTHOUSES

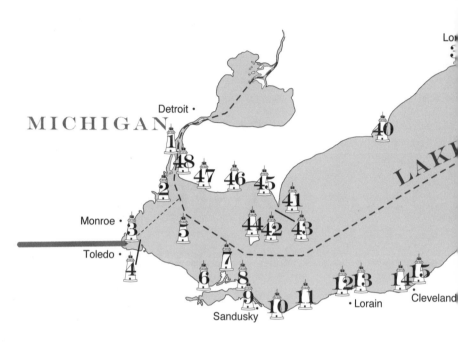

MICHIGAN

Detroit ·

Monroe ·

Toledo ·

Sandusky

· Lorain

Cleveland

OHIO

1 Grosse Ile North
   Channel Front Range
   Light
2 Detroit River
3 Toledo Harbor
4 Turtle Island
5 West Sister Island
6 Old Port Clinton Pier
7 South Bass Island
8 Marblehead
   (Sandusky)

9 Sandusky Harbor
   Pierhead (Cedar Point)
10 Huron Harbor
11 Vermilion
12 Lorain West
   Breakwater
13 Lorain East
   Breakwater
14 Cleveland West
   Breakwater

15 Cleveland East
   Pierhead
16 Fairport Harbor West
17 Old Fairport Main
   (Grand River)
18 Ashtabula
19 Erie Pierhead
20 Presque Isle
21 Erie Land
22 Barcelona
23 Dunkirk

THE LIGHTS OF LAKE ERIE

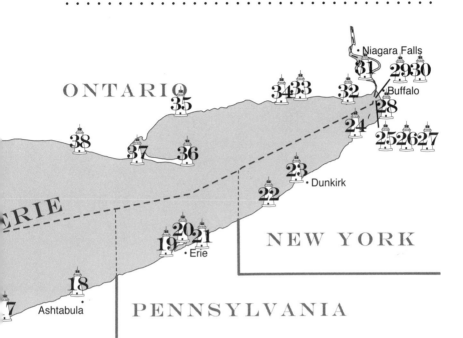

4 South Buffalo
  Southside

5 Buffalo Breakwater

6 Buffalo Breakwater
  (Leaning)

7 Buffalo Breakwater
  (Old Bottle Light)

8 Buffalo Main

9 Buffalo Lightship
  (Lightvessel No. 82)

0 Horseshoe Reef

31 Grand Island Old
  Front Range

32 Point Abino

33 Mohawk Island

34 Port Maitland Front
  Range

35 Port Dover

36 Long Point

37 Long Point West End
  (Old Cut)

38 Port Burwell

39 Port Stanley

40 Erieau East Pier

41 First Southeast Shoal
  Lightship (Kewanee)

42 Southeast Shoal

43 Pelee Passage

44 Pelee Island

45 Leamington Light

46 Kingsville

47 Colchester Reef

48 Bois Blanc (Bob-Lo)

LAKE ERIE

I n the last half of the 20th Century, Lake Erie has been widely mis-represented as the most polluted of the Great Lakes, and in popular media made sport of by persons who have never stuck a toe into its sweet waters. In fact, because it is the most shallow of the Great Lakes, it contains less volume of water and is thus the quickest of the lakes to exchange its water. As a result, the whole of Lake Erie's water is replaced in about a decade while Lake Superior, for example, being larger and deeper, takes more than a century to "flush" its water. The result is that with the decline of American heavy industry in the Great Lakes region, combined with the environmental regulations placed upon the remaining industries in the last 25 years, Lake Erie is becoming one of the cleanest waterways in the nation.

Interestingly, the scourge of Lake Erie is not man-made pollution, but man-transferred wildlife. With the careless flushing of a single ballast tank of a salt water vessel that visited the lakes via the seaway, the zebra muscle was introduced to the Great Lakes. This barnacle-like crustacean has no natural enemies in the fresh water seas and has multiplied at an exponential rate. Now, Lake Erie's shallow depths have become the breeding ground for this pest as they clog intake pipes, slow vessels and destroy shipwrecks sites that have been preserved on the bottomlands for more than a century. As of this writing, no solution to the zebra muscle problem is known. In one final twist, the zebra mussel's consumption of microscopic organisms and vegetation that reside in the lake has actually made Lake Erie even cleaner!

Oddly, Lake Erie was the last of the five lakes to be discovered by the Europeans. Until 1669, the territory was the turf of the warrior people of the mighty Iroquois Tribe. So fierce were these tribesmen that no European settlers dared to cross their borders. As a result, exploration went north and west to avoid the Iroquois and Lake Erie was left alone.

The city of Buffalo, New York marks the lakes' easternmost boundary with Toledo, Ohio marking the western limit. Along the Erie shore, the boom-towns of the industrial revolution sprung up in the places where the ore from the northern iron ranges could be dropped off and smelted into steel. The iron ore transfer cities of Cleveland, Ashtabula, Lorain and Erie all grew with the need for steel. Now, as the Twentieth Century winds down, the steel Meccas have been largely abandoned to become rust-belt.

With the industrial revolution's need for steel and ore also came a need for lakeboats to transport the raw materials. As a result, vessel traffic on Lake Erie grew with the nation's hunger for steel. To support this increase in navigation came a growth in navigational aids. This meant the construction of lighthouses, lots of them. But, with the decline in the Great Lakes steel industry came a decline in navigation and a resultant closure of many of the light facilities. Now, many of the lights rust away, like the commerce that they once aided.

1 Grosse Ile North Channel Front Range Light

☐ Visited on

_____

Established: (1894) 1906
Status: Inactive
Location: (MI) Lower Detroit River
Type: Octagonal wooden tower
Access: Boat
About the Light: *This structure is in remarkably good condition, considering that it was constructed in 1906. Standing 40 feet tall, the lighthouse was deactivated in 1963 and is currently the property of the Grosse Ile Historical Society. The other tower in this range is reported as being "lost" prior to 1940.*

2 Detroit River

☐ Visited on

_____

Established: 1885
Status: Active
Location: (MI) Southern mouth of the Detroit River
Type: Conical, cast iron
Access: Boat
About the Light: *Iron plated, this 49-foot-tall light marks the point where the busy channel of the Detroit River meets Lake Erie's steamboat tracks. When this light was first established, few lakeboats could be found that were sized in excess of 300 feet. Today, oreboats that stretch beyond 1,000 feet in length pass by the light. In the mid 1880s, the mariners looked up from the deck at the light. Now the modern mariners actually look down as they pass by!*

3 Toledo Harbor

☐ Visited on

_____

Established: 1904
Status: Active
Location: (OH) Maumee Bay
Type: Conical/integral
Access: Boat
About the Light: *One of the most unusual and eye-catching lighthouses on the Great Lakes, this structure is officially described as "Romanesque." The roof of the dwelling seems to catch your attention long before the flashing of the light. Rounded eaves melt atop the buff-colored brick house. The whole gingerbread, fairy-tale structure looks strangely out of place in the front yard of the industrial revolution. Automated in 1965, the light is an active Coast Guard facility with no access to the public.*

4 Turtle Island

☐ Visited on

_____

Established: (1832) 1866
Status: Inactive (ruins)
Location: (OH) Four and one half miles northeast
of the mouth of the Maumee River
Type: Square
Access: Boat
About the Light: *With the construction of the Toledo Harbor light in 1904, this light was declared redundant and abandoned. Today, all that remains is the shell of the light's tower. The lantern room and light are long gone, and this brick structure is suffering from the elements. The site is on an island and is accessed only by use of a boat.*

5 West Sister Island

☐ Visited on

_____

Established: 1848
Status: Active
Location: (OH) Southwest end of the island
Type: Conical, rough stone
Access: Boat
About the Light: *Only the tower remains because the lantern room and lens have been replaced by a 300mm plastic light. Other than the white stone tower, there is little else about this site to attract attention. Since the light is located almost nine miles from the nearest land, a visit is recommended to only those with the greatest of interest and spare time as well as a boat.*

6 Old Port Clinton Pier

☐ Visited on

_____

Established: 1900
Status: Inactive
Location: (OH) North shore of Portage River, west of draw-bridge.
Type: Pyramidal wooden tower
Access: Car
About the Light: *On the grounds of a private marina, but polite visitors are welcome. Just south of Highway 163.*

7 South Bass Island

☐ Visited on
_____

Established: 1897
Status: Inactive
Location: (OH) Southwest end of South Bass Island
Type: Square/integral, brick
Access: Boat
About the Light: *All of this light and its keeper's quarters are owned by the Ohio State University and are currently used as a research facility. It is considered private property, and not opened to the public. The optic has been removed from the tower* which stands 60 feet high. *The entire structure is framed of red-brick and is in excellent condition at age 100.*

8 Marblehead (Sandusky)

☐ Visited on
_____

Established: 1821
Status: Active
Location: (OH) Entrance to Sandusky Bay
Type: Conical, rough stone
Access: Car
About the Light: *Being 65 feet tall, this white tower is made of stone and uses a plastic lens to refract its beam across the lake. Nearby, a Victorian keeper's quarters stands. Even though this is an active station, the grounds are open to the public. Driving on Ohio Route 2, exit on Ohio Route 53 north and then head east on Route 163, 8 miles to the lighthouse. This is the oldest light in continuous operation on the Great Lakes. The old Fresnel lens is on display in the Marblehead Coast Guard Station.*

9 Sandusky Harbor Pierhead (Cedar Point)

☐ Visited on
_____

Established: (1839) 1935
Status: Active
Location: (OH) End of detached breakwall
Type: Skeletal
Access: Boat
About the Light: Other than a rusting skeletal tower that boosts this light some 55 feet above the lake, there is not much to see at this site. The current optic is a simple 375mm plastic lens, and this is an active aid to navigation. This site is not open to the public.

10 Huron Harbor

☐ Visited on

_____

Established: (1835) 1936
Status: Active
Location: (OH) North end of west pier
Type: "Arts Decoratifs," or art deco
Access: Car/then foot
About the Light: *Like many of the lights constructed in the 1930s era, this one has the distinctive art deco style. This site reportedly never had a lantern room, and currently has only a fixed position 375mm optic.*

11 Vermilion

☐ Visited on

_____

Established: (1835, 1877) 1991
Status: replica; private aid to navigation
Location: (OH) Inland Seas Museum
Type: Octagonal steel
Access: Car
About the Light: *This replica of the 1877 Vermilion light is just one of many sights worth seeing in the port village of Vermilion, Ohio. The maritime museum itself is one of the best, if not THE best, on the Great Lakes. From the gift shop where a person can obtain nearly everything ever written on the lakes to the library, where you actually can obtain everything written about the lakes, this museum will take an entire day to visit. When visiting Vermilion itself, lake buffs will wish that they were born and raised there. No trip to Lake Erie should miss Vermilion.*

12 Lorain West Breakwater

☐ Visited on

_____

Established: (1836) 1917
Status: Active
Location: (OH) West harbor breakwater.
Type: Square/integral, steel and concrete
Access: Boat
About the Light: *Decommissioned in 1966, the site was slated for demolition by the Coast Guard, and the effort to preserve the lighthouse has been going on since then. Interested persons can write to the "Port of Lorain Foundation, Room 511, 200 West Erie Ave., Lorain, Ohio 44052." This is a non-profit group that needs all of the help that it can get.*

13 Lorain East Breakwater

☐ Visited on
_____

Established: 1965
Status: Active
Location: (OH) End of east breakwater
Type: Square steel tower
Access: Boat
About the Light: *This light is the intended modern replacement for the 1917 light on the opposite breakwater.*

14 Cleveland West Breakwater

☐ Visited on
_____

Established: 1911
Status: Active
Location: (OH) West pierhead of Cleveland breakwall
Type: Conical, cast iron
Access: Boat
About the Light: *Automated in 1965, this brick and cast iron structure stands 67 feet above Lake Erie. Attached to the tower is a fog signal building constructed in 1910. The whole structure is an active Coast Guard facility and so is not open to the public.*

15 Cleveland East Pierhead

☐ Visited on
_____

Established: 1910
Status: Active
Location: (OH) East end of east pier
Type: Conical, cast iron
Access: Boat
About the Light: *Constructed of iron plate, this lighthouse was designed to stand for many years against the power of the lake. It was automated in 1959 and is currently solar-powered. The tower stands 25 feet above the breakwall and has a focal plane of 31 feet. Originally the light was equipped with a Fifth Order Fresnel optic, but now has only a 300mm plastic lens. This light is isolated on the breakwall and is best viewed from a boat.*

16 Fairport Harbor West

☐ Visited on
_____

Established: 1925
Status: Active
Location: (OH) On the west Fairport breakwater
Type: Square/integral, steel and concrete
Access: Boat
About the Light: *When the lamp of this light first burned in 1925, it made the old light ashore obsolete. Today this lighthouse still serves its intended function by guiding lakeboats safely into Fairport harbor. Since this is an active Coast Guard light station, trespassing is frowned upon. Standing 42 feet high, the light is equipped with a 300mm optic which has replaced its original Fourth Order optic. It is automated.*

17 Old Fairport Main (Grand River)

☐ Visited on
_____

Established: (1825) 1871
Status: Inactive; museum
Location: (OH) Inside Grand River
Type: Conical, sandstone
Access: Car
About the Light: *As it should be, this historic light is part of a local maritime museum. The existing tower was constructed in1871. Made of sandstone bricks, the tower stands 69 feet tall and has its keeper's quarters attached. It is the keeper's quarters in which the maritime museum has been established. By taking Ohio Route 2 to Fairport Road, the Old Fairport light can be accessed.*

18 Ashtabula

☐ Visited on
_____

Established: (1836, 1876, 1905) 1916
Status: Active
Location: (OH) North end of west Ashtabula breakwater
Type: Integral.square, steel and concrete
Access: Boat
About the Light: *Moved to its present location in 1916, the current light was automated in 1976. The light tower itself stands 40 feet above the lake and is constructed of steel and iron plate. This site is an operational facility administered by the U.S. Coast Guard and so is not open to the public. A light buff keen on getting close to the structure to view or photograph it would have to go by boat.*

19 Erie Pierhead

Visited on
_____

Established: 1857
Status: Active
Location: (PA) East end of north pier, Presque Isle State Park
Type: Square tapering tower
Access: Car
About the Light: *This 30' tower has been moved twice, the last move in the 1940s when it was moved to its present location. Early in this century the light was located on the grounds of the US Life Saving station, just east of the current US Coast Guard station. During the 1940 reconstruction the tower was boxed in with heavy steel plating. It was originally fitted with a fourth order Fresnel lens, the light now displays a fixed, flashing red light emitted by a modern plastic lens.*

20 Presque Isle

Visited on
_____

Established: 1873
Status: Active
Location: (PA) Northern tip of Presque Isle Peninsula
Type: Square/integral brick tower and dwelling
Access: Car
About the Light: *The Presque Isle light has been standing guard for 125 years. Constructed of brick, the light is now used as the residence for the manager of Presque Isle Park. Access can be gained by driving PA Route 5 and exiting at Peninsula Drive. Follow the drive and enter the state park.*

21 Erie Land

Visited on
_____

Established: (1818) 1867
Status: Inactive
Location: (PA) In Erie at north end of Lighthouse Street
Type: Conical, sandstone
Access: Car
About the Light: *Said to be one of the first lights on Lake Erie, this light is in remarkably good condition considering that it was deactivated in 1900! To access the site, drive along PA Route 5, Alternate (Lake Road East) and head north on, of course, Lighthouse Street. The lantern room and watch rooms are wooden reproductions built in 1989.*

22 Barcelona

☐ Visited on

_____

Established: 1829
Status: Inactive; private residence
Location: (NY) Just north of New York Route 394 on New York Route 5
Type: Conical, rough stone
Access: Car
About the Light: *Local boulders and stones were used to construct the tower for this light, and it is said to be the first light in the nation to be powered by natural gas. Today, only the stone tower is intact and the lamp facility is missing. As a private residence, the site is not open to the public and can only be viewed from the road.*

23 Dunkirk

☐ Visited on

_____

Established: (1827) 1875
Status: Active
Location: (NY) On the end of Gratiot Point, west of Dunkirk Harbor
Type: Square limestone tower with brick dwelling attached
Access: Car
About the Light: *This brick tower is a part of a local military museum which has been established in the nearby light keeper's quarters. To access the site, take Lake Shore Drive and exit at Point Drive North. The light tower is open to the public and the determined light buff can actually climb the tower and view the blue expanse of Lake Erie.*

24 South Buffalo Southside

☐ Visited on

_____

Established: 1903
Status: Inactive
Location: (NY) Industrial breakwater at south harbor entrance
Type: Conical, cast iron
Access: Boat
About the Light: *For a lighthouse that is located in one of the most densely populated parts of the Great Lakes, this site is one of the most secluded. The light is located on private property and is flanked by long-standing industrial facilities. Access is difficult by any means other than a healthy boat. This light was automated in 1935 and has a focal plane of 40 feet. Or if you wish, view from NY Route 5 on southern approach into Buffalo.*

25 Buffalo Breakwater

☐ Visited on
_____

Established: 1961
Status: Active
Location: (NY) End of outer detached breakwater
Type: Octagonal steel tower
Access: Boat
About the Light: _This 71-foot-tall was constructed to replace the 1872 lighthouse (below) after it was knocked off its foundation in 1958 by the freighter FRONTENAC._

26 Buffalo Breakwater (Leaning)

☐ Visited on
_____

Established: 1872
Status: Demolished
Location: (NY) Formerly on the outer breakwater
Type: Integral
Access: None
About the Light: _A need for an additional navigation aid caused the construction of this light in 1872 as a supplement to the inner harbor light. It performed that task until 1958 when the 600 foot oreboat FRONTENAC smacked into the structure while attempting to turn. The impact knocked the entire lighthouse off its foundation and gave it a 16 degree lean! Three years later a modern steel "skeleton" light replaced the now famous "leaning lighthouse of Buffalo" and shortly thereafter the original structure was torn down. Great Lakes Historical Society photo._

27 Buffalo Breakwater (Old Bottle Light)

☐ Visited on
_____

Established: 1903
Status: Inactive
Location: (NY) On display near main light
Type: Bottle shaped, conical cast iron
Access: Car/ then foot
About the Light: _This unique light was constructed of boiler plate cast-iron and planted on the breakwall. The Jules Verne shape is reminiscent of the era in which it was constructed and gives the impression that someone may be placed inside and lowered to 20,000 leagues under the sea. In 1985, the light was deactivated and later moved to its present location as part of the Dunkirk Historical Lighthouse and Veterans Park museum complex._

28 Buffalo Main

☐ Visited on

_____

Established: (1818) 1833
Status: Inactive
Location: (NY) At the mouth of the Buffalo River
Type: Octagonal limestone
Access: Car

About the Light: *Originally the need for a light at this location was filled by a beacon constructed in 1818. Because the first light was found to be too dim, the existing tower was erected to replace that light in 1833. The octagonal tower is constructed of neatly-carved stone blocks set in place to withstand many centuries. This tower is both a landmark and a treasure of the Great Lakes. Getting to the light requires very little effort. Take New York Route 5 "Skyway" exit at Fuhrmann Boulevard and follow the signs leading to the Coast Guard station. The light is located adjacent to the station property and is part of an outdoor museum.*

No photo available.

29 Buffalo Lightship

☐ Visited on

_____

Established: 1912
Status: Lost at sea
Location: (NY) 13 miles west of Buffalo in Lake Erie
Type: Steel
Access: History books

About the Light: *Anchored to the bottom of Lake Erie, Lightvessel No. 82 was the first marker on the approach to the bustling port of Buffalo. On November 10, 1913, however, a monster autumn gale arrived on Lake Erie. This famed storm, often referred to as "The great storm of 1913" had ravaged lakes Michigan, Superior and Huron. Giant lakeboats had already been sent to the bottom with all hands by the time the storm hit the one year old LIGHTVESSEL No. 82. It too was sent to the bottom with all six of its crew. The following spring the lightship was found, raised and returned to service where it operated until 1936.*

30 Horseshoe Reef

☐ Visited on

_____

Established: 1856
Status: Inactive; ruins
Location: (NY) On the reef, one and one half miles east of Buffalo
Type: Wood
Access: Boat

About the Light: *This light once marked a reef that has always been a hazard to the navigation of the port city of Buffalo. Keeper's lived ashore and used boats to tend to the light. In 1920, the Buffalo Crib Light made this light redundant and it was abandoned. The winds and waves have since destroyed all but the steel support skeleton. Other than the gulls, there is not much of interest remaining at this site.*

31 Grand Island Old Front Range

☐ Visited on

_____

Established: 1917
Status: Inactive
Location: (NY)
Type: Octagonal wooden tower
Access: Car
About the Light: *Now on the grounds of a private marina, but polite visitors are welcome.*

32 Point Abino

☐ Visited on

_____

Established: 1917
Status: Active
Location: (ONT) Tip of Point Abino
Type: Square, concrete reinforced
Access: Car
About the Light: *Erected as a replacement for the Buffalo Lightship which was sunk with all hands in the "Great Storm of 1913," this light remains active. Painted red and white, the concrete structure appears to be constructed with fighting off the lake in mind. The site is on property that is not open to the public and although it can be reached by car, a pass with a motorboat may be the best way to see it. This light was also featured in the 1995 made-for-T.V. movie "Lady Killer."*

33 Mohawk Island

☐ Visited on

_____

Established: 1848
Status: Inactive; ruins
Location: (ONT) South side of Mohawk Island
Type: Conical, limestone
Access: Boat
About the Light: *By the early 1930s, this light was on the way to obsolescence. Lake traffic in the depression years was dwindling in this region and the route that led to the Welland Canal was moved a greater distance from this lighthouse. Then in 1932, the keeper and his son were trapped in the ice while leaving the light at the end of the season and froze to death. The next season the light was automated and later replaced by a lighted buoy. Today the light is abandoned and in a bad state of decay. Soon it will probably be claimed by Lake Erie just like its last keeper.*

34 Port Maitland Front Range

☐ Visited on

_____

Established: 1830
Status: Active
Location: (ONT) South end of west pier
Type: Pyramidal wooden tower, aluminum sided
Access: Car
About the Light:

35 Port Dover

☐ Visited on

_____

Established: 1846
Status: Active
Location: (ONT) South end of west pier
Type: Pyramidal wooden tower, aluminum sided
Access: Car
About the Light:

36 Long Point

☐ Visited on

_____

Established: (1830, 1843) 1916
Status: Active
Location: (ONT) East end of Long Point
Type: Octagonal reinforced concrete
Access: Boat/Helicopter
About the Light: *This light is an active station as well as being deep into a National Wildlife Area. Because of those reasons, the lighthouse is nearly inaccessible. The concrete tower is painted bright white. A keeper's quarters was once located near the light, but after the light was solar-powered and automated, the quarters fell to ruins.*

37 Long Point West End (Old Cut)

☐ Visited on _____

Established: 1879
Status: Inactive; private residence
Location: (ONT) On the northwest shore of Long Point
Type: Pyramidal wooded tower
Access: Car
About the Light: *This light originally marked the "cut" channel through Long Point. By the beginning of the 1900s, however, the point had grown and the cut was filled in by nature and soon the light was no longer needed. Today the lighthouse is a private residence and is not open to the public. It is located on the highway immediately west of Long Point Provincial Park.*

38 Port Burwell

☐ Visited on _____

Established: 1840
Status: Inactive; museum
Location: (ONT) East mouth of Otter Creek
Type: Octagonal wooden tower
Access: Car
About the Light: *Rare are the lighthouses that are constructed of wood, but this is one of them. Standing 65 feet tall, this site is well cared for by the local residents and was completely restored in 1986.. Adjacent to the light is a maritime museum where the lens of the lighthouse can be seen. To get there, take Highway 42 and exit at Robinson Street and drive toward Lake Erie.*

39 Port Stanley

☐ Visited on _____

Established: 1908
Status: Active
Location: (ONT) End of west pier
Type: Reinforced concrete
Access: Car
About the Light:

40 Erieau East Pier

☐ Visited on

_____

Established:
Status: Active
Location: (ONT) End of east pier
Type: Skeletal
Access: Car
About the Light:

No photo
available.

41 First Southeast Shoal Lightship Established: 1901

☐ Visited on

_____

Status: Removed
Location: (ONT) Southeast Shoal
Type: Lightship
Access: None
About the Light: _The threat of the Southeast Shoal grew with the increase of lake shipping prior to the 1900s. Southeast Shoal, however, was in Canadian waters and the government there did not see fit to locate a light in that area. The United States Lighthouse Board, on the other hand, said that the site was in Canadian waters and not their problem. As a compromise, the Lake Carriers Association chartered this lightship to guard the shoal. On June 5th, 1910, the private lightship was replaced by a Canadian government vessel. Today a "heli-pad type" light is in this place._

42 Southeast Shoal

☐ Visited on

_____

Established: 1920s
Status: Active
Location: (ONT) Southeast Shoal
Type: Square reinforced concrete
Access: Boat
About the Light: _This shoal extends southward over a mile into the lake from Point Pelee, Ontario, to the north into a very busy shipping channel along the north shore. This location was originally marked by a Lightship._

58

43 Pelee Passage

Established: (1861, 1902) 1975
Status: Active
Location: (ONT) Middle Ground Shoal, northeast of Pelee Island
Type: Modern steel and concrete
Access: Boat
About the Light: *Middle Ground Shoal extends northward from Pelee Island into a busy shipping channel. This is the third light to mark this shoal.*

☐ Visited on
_____

44 Pelee Island

Established: 1833
Status: Ruins
Location: (ONT) Northeastern tip of Pelee Island
Type: Conical, rough stone
Access: Ferry to the island
About the Light: *Sometimes the ruins of an old site are just as much fun as a restored site. Such is the case with the Pelee Island light. Its rough stone tower is all that remains. Deactivated in 1909, the lantern room and windows are all long gone. Even though the structure as it stands invokes a romantic era, there is currently a move afoot by the citizens of Canada to completely restore the light.*

☐ Visited on
_____

45 Leamington Light

Established: 1940s
Status: Inactive; privately owned
Location: (ONT) Northwest of main harbor
Type: Pyramidal, wooden tower
Access: Car
About the Light: *Built as a private aid to navigation prior to the expansion of the modern harbor. Currently located within a private residential area known as the Lighthouse Club.*

☐ Visited on
_____

46 Kingsville

☐ Visited on
_____

Established: 1900
Status: Inactive
Location: (ONT) Exhibit area behind Royal Canadian Legion Hall
Type: Pyramidal wooden tower
Access: Car
About the Light: _Moved to this site and restored as part of an outdoor exhibit when the modern structure was put into service._

47 Colchester Reef

☐ Visited on
_____

Established: 1885
Status: Active
Location: (ONT) Colchester Reef, five miles southeast of Colchester, Ontario
Type: Skeletal
Access: Boat
About the Light: _Like many lights in the lake, this one fell in the area where Canada owned the lake, but the United States owned most of the vessel traffic. At first, a lightship was placed in this position. After the lightship was swallowed by the lake, the Canadian Government elected to build a light in its place. Today the light-tower has been cut down to a helipad with a plastic lens attached. SEE STORY ON PAGE 61._

48 Bois Blanc (Bob-Lo)

☐ Visited on
_____

Established: 1839
Status: Inactive; ruins, privately owned
Location: (MI) Southeast tip of Bois Blanc Island
Type: Conical, rough stone
Access: Boat
About the Light: _This light originally marked the southern tip of Bois Blanc Island in the southern Detroit River. Modern aids to navigation soon over-populated the area and this light was deactivated. Today all that remains is the stone tower. Both the island and the light are privately owned and are being developed for residential use._

THE CAMBELL BROTHERS'
MYSTERY LIGHTSHIP

In the mid 1800s, the science of navigation on the Great Lakes was not really a science at all. It has always been said by salt water sailors that the Great Lakes mariners navigate around the freshwater seas by the method of "Dog-barking." This is the contention that every lakeboat has a dog aboard, and every house and farm along the rivers and shores of the lakes also has a dog in the yard. So close is the Great Lakes community that every boat dog knows every shore dog and when one dog barks to another, the mariners know by the barks where to turn and thus can navigate in thick weather without the use of charts.

Although the "Dog-barking" concept is nothing more then a Paunt-water sailor's slam at the crude navigational methods supposedly used by their Great Lakes counter-parts, it is sometimes closer to reality than many would like to admit. In the early years of the lake maritime industry, charts and navigation aids were often home-made. Traditionally, the powers of national government have relegated the Great Lakes to the bottom of the list when waiting for services. The high seas get the meat from the federal kitchen and the lakes get the scraps. Until the 1870s, this was even true of the lighthouse board. The circumstances of home-made and second-rate aids to navigation were worse yet in Canadian waters. Charts were often highly inaccurate and many aids to navigation were owned by private citizens. A case in point was the Colchester Reef Light.

Colchester Reef is a spot where the shallows of Lake Erie get very shallow indeed. To make matters worse, the reef is practically on the doorstep of the Detroit River. For almost two centuries, vessels that headed across the Great

Lakes had to squeeze through Pelee Passage to find the mouth of the mighty river, and the northwest boundary of that passage is marked by the submerged rocks of Colchester Reef. Lake mariners, for many years, relied on

memory and hand-written notes on their charts to mark the reef, but the shelf of shallows seemed to move – and claimed many vessels. In fact, the reef was not moving, but the location was marked by speculation alone. Making the zigzag courses between Pelee Island and Point Pelee, vessels were deprived of good reference, having only the Pointe Pelee lighthouse on the north tip of Pelee Island to sight upon. The result was that the zigzag had to be accomplished by guesswork alone. If the vessel was as little as eight degrees off course, it would run smack onto the reef. Considering that little more than line of sight was used in this operation, it was clear that something needed to be done about the reef.

There was little willingness on the part of the Canadian government to place a navigation light on this spot. Hearing the cries of the maritime community, the Canadians did come up with an inexpensive solution, however. The firm of Cambell Brothers and Company negotiated a contract with the Canadian Government for the placement of a lightship on the reef. Records of the lightship itself are sparse in the extreme, and there is no account yet found by this author as to exactly when the lightship went on station. Also there is no written record of the lightvessel's type or configuration, but a good guess would be that the boat was a small wooden schooner with a light that could be hoisted to the

The Colchester Reef Lightship, circa 1883.

– Author's Drawing

top of its mast. This conclusion is drawn from the assertion that the Cambell brothers were probably the lowest bidders and looking to gain as much profit as possible from their government contract.

Most reports indicate that the Colchester Reef lightship went on station in the early 1870s. Probably in 1881, the vessel was put in the charge of Captain Forrest, who was its sole crewmember. Apparently, the deal between the Canadian Government and the Cambell brothers rapidly went sour because, for reasons that only they knew for certain, the Cambell's suddenly removed their lightship from its station without any type of public notice. This action took place in late September of 1881, and instantly caused trouble. In the first hours of Sunday, September 25th, the steamer ANTELOPE came huffing westbound from Buffalo with a three barge tow. When the steamer had made her downbound passage a few days earlier, the home-made lightship was on her station atop Colchester Reef just like she had been on previous trips. On the way back up, Captain Bule, the ANTELOPE's master, had no idea at all that the lightship had been removed. Zigzagging his steamer through Pelee Passage, Captain Bule sighted a bright white light to the northwest that he assumed to be the lightship, but was in fact another vessel that was at anchor well north of the reef. In the wee hours of the night and with a gale blowing, the captain did exactly what he should have done, he used the distant light to set his course. Navigating on that light, the good captain was lured into a collision with the reef which nearly destroyed the ANTELOPE.

Later that same day, with the ANTELOPE still fetched up in the reef, the Cambell brothers had their lightship returned to Colchester Reef. Once in place, however, it was found that the hoisting gear for raising the light to the top of the mast would not work, thus forcing Captain Forrest to shine the light from deck level, which made it almost useless. Indeed, the Cambell's had apparently supplied the lowest grade of equipment for their contract lightship. Once again the night passed and the reef was not properly marked.

For the next two years, the Cambell's light was used to mark Colchester Reef. Then came the second week of November 1883, and a screaming gale that swept the Great Lakes on the 11th and 12th of that month. When the storm cleared, the Colchester Reef lightship and Captain Forrest were both missing. There begins the mystery of the Cambell brothers' lightship. Among the published accounts and historic records, very little is mentioned of the fate of the lightship or that of Captain Forrest; they are simply written off with the minor storm notes. The conclusion to the tale was set in the pages of history with the following casual report over the wire services:

> *"Ottawa, Ont., Nov.15 – The government has decided not to replace the Colchester Reef lightship this season, as still weather is necessary in order to accomplish it and such weather is not likely to occur again before navigation closes."*

There is no word as to the final disposition of the lightship or its master, and the exact ending of this tale remains a mystery. Did Captain Forrest manage to direct his lightship to some safe place amid one of the worst storms in Great Lakes history, or were both consumed by Lake Erie? As of this writing we are still working on that question.

In 1885 a lighthouse was constructed on Colchester Reef, and today that light's tower base is the foundation for a heli-pad. Atop the heli-pad is an automated light that marks the reef. Even in modern times, this is a hazardous place for lakeboats, and the Colchester Reef light is an important aid to navigation. Unfortunately, all that exists of the Colchester Reef lightship is printed here, and there is nothing else but questions remaining.

THE
LIGHTS
OF LAKE
ST. CLAIR

THE LIGHTS OF LAKE ST. CLAIR

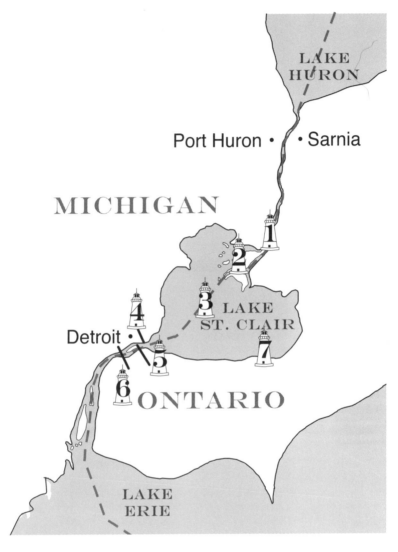

1 Peche Island

2 St. Clair Flats Old
  Channel Ranges

3 Lake St. Clair

4 Windmill Point

5 William Livingstone
  Memorial

6 Detroit Lighthouse Depot

7 Thames River Rear Range

1 Peche Island

☐ Visited on
_____

Established: 1908
Status: Inactive; display
Location: (MI) Marine City waterfront
Type: Conical, cast iron
Access: Car
About the Light: *Originally placed as a range light at Peche Island near Belle Isle, this light had its foundation washed away and was leaning toward collapse. In the early 1980s the light was de-commissioned and replaced, but was rescued and taken to a water-front park in Marine City, Michigan on the banks of the St. Clair River. The conical tower is skirted in steel plate and has atop it a Sixth Order Fresnel lens, one of few remaining on the Great Lakes.*

2 St. Clair Flats Front Channel Range

☐ Visited on
_____

Established: (1859) 1875
Status: Active
Location: (MI) Mouth of St. Clair River, old south channel
Type: Conical, yellow brick
Access: Boat
About the Light: *This pair of brick light towers were established to aid vessels in aligning the course between Lake St. Clair and the St. Clair River. Now badly weathered, it is equipped with simple plastic lens in place of its original optics. In the early 1870s, the front light developed a bad lean and appeared about to fall over. In 1875 the light was re-cribbed, but today the light is leaning again but is currently being restored.*

2 St. Clair Flats Rear Channel Range

☐ Visited on
_____

Established: 1859
Status: Inactive; ruins
Location: (MI) Mouth of St. Clair River, old south channel
Type: Conical, yellow brick
Access: Boat
About the Light: *The second light in the pair of range lights, this tower has the same basic history as its twin. Access to this site is by boat, but not recommended as the swift current and general condition of the towers make it a very hazardous place.*

71

3 Lake St. Clair

☐ Visited on

_____

Established: 1941
Status: Active
Location: (MI) Lake St. Clair, bend in mid-lake shipping channel
Type: Cylindrical steel and concrete
Access: Boat
About the Light: *This light is a modern pillar-with-a-lamp-on-it structure that replaced an earlier Lightship. It has a focal plane of 53 feet and is made of steel. The site is an active aid to navigation and so is not open to the public.*

4 Windmill Point

☐ Visited on

_____

Established: (1833, 1866, 1875, 1891) 1933
Status: Active
Location: (MI) Head of Detroit River at foot of Alter Road
Type: Conical steel plate
Access: Car
About the Light: *Constructed of cast iron, this light is one of the few from its era not to be built in the distinctive 1930s art deco style. Access to the light is gained by driving east Jefferson Avenue and then towards the river on Alter Road. Use caution, as the site is located near one of Detroit's not-so-nice areas.*

5 William Livingstone Memorial

☐ Visited on

_____

Established: 1929
Status: Active; memorial
Location: (MI) East end of Belle Isle, upper Detroit River
Type: Art deco style marble tower
Access: Car/then foot
About the Light: *This site is not really intended to be an aid to navigation, but is a favored place among light buffs. William Livingston was the President of the Lake Carriers' Association from 1902 until his death in 1925. This was an influential period in the lakes' maritime industry and he was a prime player. The site is a repository for one of the few remaining occulting lamps (see "What Made the Tawas Light Wink?" later in this text), and is worth visiting for that reason alone. To get there, drive to Belle Isle and stop at the Dossin Museum; foot paths will lead to the light.*

6 Detroit Lighthouse Depot

☐ Visited on
_____

Established: 1874
Status: Inactive
Location: (MI) Foot of Elliott Avenue, Detroit
Type: Brick warehouse
Access: Car
About the Light: _Formerly the central supply depot for the lighthouse activity on the lakes, this site was later transferred to the Coast Guard. It has since been abandoned by them and taken over by the City of Detroit. Plans to make it into a museum facility are pending._

7 Thames River Rear Range

☐ Visited on
_____

Established: (1818) 1867
Status: Active
Location: (ONT) Mouth of Thames River near Tilbury
Type: Conical masonry tower
Access: Car
About the Light: _A rubble-stone tower was later heightened by a brick extension in 1867. By 1970, the tower was near collapse. From 1973 to 1975, the Lower Thames Conservation Authority restored the lighthouse by dismantling it stone by stone, fixing the foundation, and then rebuilding._

73

THE
LIGHTS
OF LAKE
HURON

GREAT LAKES LIGHTHOUSES

Sault Ste. Marie

Sault Ste Marie

• Sudbury

St. Ignace

Mackinaw City

Alpena •

MICHIGAN

LAKE HURON

GEORG

BA

Port Elgin

ONT

• Bay City
• Saginaw

Port Huron • / • Sarnia

Goderich

1 Huron Lightship	6 Port Austin Reef	10 Tawas Point
2 Fort Gratiot	7 Saginaw River Rear	11 Sturgeon Point
3 Port Sanilac	Range	12 Alpena
4 Harbor Beach	8 Gravelly Shoal	13 Thunder Bay Island
5 Pointe Aux Barques	9 Charity Island	14 Middle Island

76

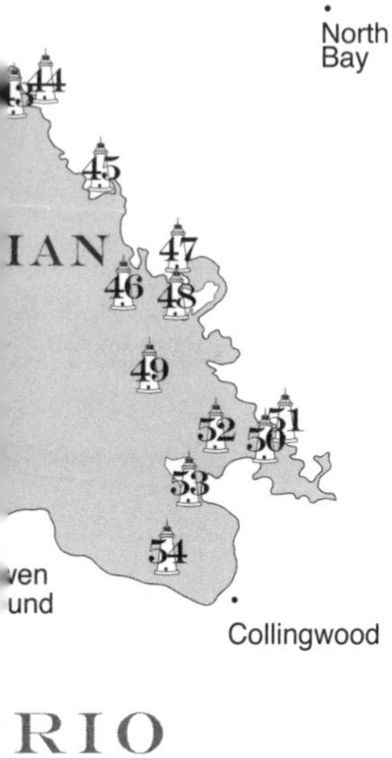

The Lights of Lake Huron

North
Bay

IAN

ven
und

Collingwood

RIO

18 Presque Isle
19 Forty Mile Point
20 Spectacle Reef
21 Poe Reef
22 Fourteen Foot Shoal
23 Bois Blanc Island
24 Cheboygan Crib
   Light
25 Cheboygan River
   Front Range
26 Old Mackinac Point
27 Round Island
28 Round Island Passage
29 Martin Reef
30 De Tour Reef
31 Shoal Island
32 Wilson Channel Front
   Range
33 Wilson Channel Rear
   Range
34 West Sister Rock
35 McKay Island
36 Mississagi Strait
37 Great Duck Island
38 Gore Bay
   (Janet Head)
39 Kagawong
40 Strawberry Island
41 Manitowaning
42 Killarney East
43 Gereaux Island
44 Byng Inlet Range

45 Pointe au Baril
46 Red Rock
47 Snug Harbour
48 Jones Island
49 Western Islands
50 Brebeuf Island
51 Beausoleil Island
52 Hope Island
53 Christian Island
54 Nottawasaga Island
55 Griffith Island
56 Cape Croker
57 Lion's Head
58 Cabot Head
59 Flowerpot Island
60 Lonely Island
61 South Baymouth
   Front Range
62 South Baymouth Rear
   Range
63 Cove Island
64 Big Tub
65 Chantry Island
66 Saugeen River Front
   Range
67 Saugeen River Rear
   Range
68 Kincardine
69 Point Clark
70 Goderich

15 Presque Isle Harbor
   Front Range
16 Presque Isle Harbor
   Rear Range
17 Old Presque Isle

The Lights of Lake Huron

Lake Huron

L ake Huron embodies all of the qualities of the entire Great Lakes chain in a single body of water. It has its densely populated high traffic area in the "pocket" region near Port Huron. A "vacation coast" runs from the thumb of Michigan up to historic Mackinac Island where the engineering marvel of the mighty Mackinac Bridge suddenly leaps out of the wooded wilderness with towers of steel. For those who seek the isolation of the great northern region, Georgian Bay hides in the eastern extreme of Lake Huron with a dimension that would allow anyone to rightly call it an individual Great Lake. In the summer Huron sparkles an indigo blue that complements the pleasure boats which dot its surface. In the winter, vast areas of the lake are covered with thick layers of ice. In the spring and fall, the lake often shows its temper pitching gale-force fits. Statistically, Lake Huron is responsible for more shipwrecks than any of the other Great Lakes. Including Lake St. Clair and the St. Clair River area, Lake Huron is the site of more than 1,300 wrecks, that is 35% of all shipping disasters on the Great Lakes! The reason for this is the complex shifting of shipping centers, products and vessel construction over the recorded history of Great Lakes commerce. As the shipping points of given products as well as the products themselves shifted around the lakes, the path leading to the ports of call seemed always to pass across Lake Huron. As the era of lake shipping began its mid 1800s boom, the era of the wooden ship also began to boom and once again, all paths seemed to lead across Lake Huron. The final result was that Lake Huron experienced the highest volume of vulnerable vessels over the greatest length of time. Lake Superior, by comparison, is far more romanced as the most treacherous of lakes, but contains only 500 shipwrecks, just over one third of Huron's toll.

GREAT LAKES LIGHTHOUSES

The lighthouses on Lake Huron reflect the lake's diverse qualities. Some are easy to access, while others are so isolated that a true pilgrimage must be planned to visit them. Many of the lights remain on guard to guide the lake mariners, while others are abandoned and rotting away. If time for a single visit is all that a light buff has to "see it all," Lake Huron is the best bet.

1 Huron Lightship

☑ Visited on
8/1/03

Established: (1920) 1935
Status: Inactive
Location: (MI) Riverside Park, Port Huron
Type: Lightvessel
Access: Car
About the Light: *This light started its career as a relief lightvessel in 1935, located at the mouth of the Port Huron River. In 1971 the boat was decommissioned while holding the title of being the last lightship on the great lakes. Today it is a museum display that is beached on the shore of the St. Clair River in Port Huron. Access is very easy, as the park is located just below the Blue Water Bridge and the lightship is nearly in the parking lot. This is one of the best spots on the lakes to go and watch the lakeboats and is also within walking distance of the Fort Gratiot lighthouse.*

2 Fort Gratiot

☑ Visited on
8/1/03

Established: (1825) 1829
Status: Active
Location: (MI) Head of the St. Clair River
Type: Conical, brick
Access: Foot
About the Light: *Located on the American side of the St. Clair River, this light is readily accessible by parking anywhere in the park above the Bluewater Bridge and following the river-walk toward Lake Huron. This 1829 tower is the oldest existing lighthouse in Michigan and is located on an active Coast Guard facility. It was increased to the present 86-foot height in 1862 and automated in 1933.*

3 Port Sanilac

☑ Visited on
8/1/03

Established: 1886
Status: Active; private residence
Location: (MI) City of Port Sanilac
Type: Octagonal, brick
Access: Car
About the Light: *Port Sanilac is another in a long chain of lake-side towns that once visited makes you wish that you lived there. Driving along M-25, the city is located just north of Lexington and is rapidly becoming a haven of tourism. Although the quarters attached to this light are private and thus the site is not open to the public, the light itself remains an active aid to navigation. The 69-foot-tall light has a beam that can be seen 16 miles out at lake level.*

4 Harbor Beach (Sand Beach)

☑ Visited on

8/1/03

Established: 1885
Status: Active
Location: (MI) Harbor Beach pierhead
Type: Conical, cast iron
Access: Boat
About the Light: *In its heyday prior to the 1900s, this port was a major harbor of refuge and was the home of one of the most active lifesaving crews on Lake Huron. In the 1880s, a massive breakwater extension was constructed and countless lakeboats took shelter. Dozens of shipwrecks lay around this area, evidence of the boats that tried, but did not make, the shelter. Today the light remains active, but the lakeboats have long ago out-grown the need for this port's shelter. Located far out on the breakwater pier, the light is nearly inaccessible. The tower is identical to that of the Detroit River light.*

5 Pointe Aux Barques

☐ Visited on

Established: (1847) 1876
Status: Active (as of this writing)
Location: (MI) North of Port Hope, tip of Michigan's thumb
Type: Conical, brick
Access: Car
About the Light: *One of the best-kept secrets on the Great Lakes is the small, rustic campgrounds that is located right at the base of this historic light. Turning off M-25 at Lighthouse Road and following it a short distance to the County Lighthouse park will take you to the campgrounds. While staying there you may have occasion to be visited by the pleasant ghost of a young lady who is said to reside at the light. Also at the light is a maritime and shipwreck museum which is worth visiting. The brick tower of this light is 89 feet tall and is, as of this writing, active.*

6 Port Austin Reef

☐ Visited on

Established: (1878) 1876
Status: Active
Location: (MI) Port Austin Reef, at the tip of Michigan's thumb.
Type: Square
Access: Boat
About the Light: *Rapidly weathering, the light no longer contains its original Fourth Order Fresnel lens, but is illuminated by a plastic lamp. Made of brick on an octagonal foundation the light is currently being renovated by the Port Austin Reef Lighthouse Association. Located almost a mile and a half from the nearest land, the best way to visit the light is by boat or by aircraft. There is a sight-seeing charter service located off M-25 near Grindstone City.*

7 Saginaw River Rear Range

☐ Visited on

Established: (1841) 1876
Status: Inactive; private ownership
Location: (MI) West bank of the mouth of the Saginaw River.
Type: Square/integral, brick
Access: Boat
About the Light: *The original light was replaced by the current brick structure in 1876, which stands 68 feet tall. Access can be gained by boat on the Saginaw River. The concept of "Range lights," or setting out two lights, one behind the other in an alignment that vessel captains could sight on, and thus by lining the lights up, line themselves up within the channel, was born here. Dewitt C. Brawn, the 15-year-old son of the keeper, brain-stormed a system where two oil lamps would be hoisted atop two towers. Inbound captains could line them up and be guided into the river. It worked. Now, the system is used all over the world!*

8 Gravelly Shoal

☐ Visited on

Established: 1939
Status: Active
Location: (MI) 2.7 miles southeast of Point Lookout
Type: "Arts Decoratifs," or art deco; steel and concrete
Access: Boat
About the Light: *Constructed as an automated remote facility, the light stands 65 feet tall on a concrete crib. The structure is made of concrete reinforced by steel. Rather than a lantern room a 300-mm lens is used in the illumination process. It is one of several "Arts Decoratifs," or art deco styled lights that were erected in the 1930s. Due to this site's remote location, access is gained by boat only. The light is an active aid to navigation and so is not open to the public. Venturing onto Point Lookout to see the light is not advisable as all of the property is taken by private residences.*

9 Charity Island

☐ Visited on

Established: 1857
Status: Ruins, privately owned
Location: (MI) Northwest tip of Big Charity Island
Type: Conical, brick with wooden dwelling
Access: Boat
About the Light: *One of the saddest Great Lakes lights, this site has stood unmanned since 1900 when it was automated from an oil light to an acetylene lamp. In 1939, the construction of the Gravelly Shoal light caused this light to be abandoned. Since then the site has fallen prey to vandals and the elements. While the 1857 site remains somewhat intact with the tower, lantern room frame and attached shell of the keeper's quarters standing it is only a matter of time, however, before some vandal sets fire to the buildings or knocks down parts of the tower, "just for kicks."*

10 Tawas Point

☐ Visited on

_____

Established: (1853) 1876
Status: Active
Location: (MI) End of Tawas Point.
Type: Conical, brick
Access: Car
About the Light: *If the Charity Island light is the sad spot on Lake Huron, Tawas Point is the bright spot. The original light was built on what was then the end of the point. By the 1870s, however, the point had grown so far out into the lake that the* light was too far inland to be of use. The current light was built in 1875. Today the light is an active Coast Guard facility which is open to the public on weekends. If the light is kept in the same manner as this spotless park, the light is insured of long, safe and happy preservation. SEE STORY ON PAGE 105.

11 Sturgeon Point

☐ Visited on

_____

Established: 1870
Status: Active
Location: (MI) Tip of Sturgeon Point
Type: Conical, brick
Access: Car
About the Light: *Although somewhat easy to miss, this light is one of the few that a visitor can climb and so should not miss! Exit US-23 north of Harrisville on Point Road. Follow it to the light. A terrific little maritime museum exists in the keeper's* quarters, with a gift shop in a building in the rear. The brick tower stands 68 feet tall and contains a Third and a Half Order Optic. Although automated, the light is very well kept and is currently planned for decommissioning. If decommissioning occurs, the status of the site is said to continue as it is.

12 Alpena

☐ Visited on

_____

Established: (1875, 1878) 1914
Status: Active
Location: (MI) Mouth of Thunder Bay River
Type: Skeletal
Access: Car
About the Light: *This light is little more than a lamp on a skeletal tower. The focal plane of the light is measured at 64 feet and its original Fourth* Order optic has been replaced with a 190mm plastic lens. The site is an active aid to navigation and is not open to the public.

13 Thunder Bay Island

☐ Visited on _____

Established: 1832
Status: Active
Location: (MI) Southeast end of Thunder Bay Island
Type: Conical, rough stone
Access: Boat
About the Light: *The island on which this light is located is just outside of Thunder Bay itself and is four miles off shore. This light has a rather odd shape with its bottom third sloping at a greater angle than the top two thirds, as it was raised 10 feet in 1857. Knowing that the station was automated in 1983, it seems amazing that this isolated light was occupied for so long. The house dates from 1868, and the facility is currently undergoing restoration.*

14 Middle Island

☐ Visited on _____

Established: 1905
Status: Active
Location: (MI) 10 miles north of Alpena and four miles off shore on the east side of Middle Island
Type: Conical, brick
Access: Boat
About the Light: *Once an abandoned site, this light has been taken over by the Middle Island Light Keeper's Association. Members of the association pitch in and are restoring the site to its post 1905 appearance. The idea is to turn the keeper's quarters into a bed and breakfast.*

15 Presque Isle Harbor Front Range

☐ Visited on _____

Established: 1870
Status: Inactive
Location: (MI) Presque Isle, at entrance to old 1840 lighthouse museum
Type: Short octagonal tower, wood
Access: Car
About the Light: *Part of a two house range, this light is a piece in the sprawling lighthouse park in Presque Isle. The structure is wood-framed and is accessible to the public. Driving along US-23, you will find this part of Michigan's shore, a light buff's dream, just north of Alpena. It was moved to the current site when replaced by a modern structure.*

16 Presque Isle Harbor Rear Range

☐ Visited on
_____

Established: 1870
Status: Inactive; private residence
Location: (MI) SW shore of harbor
Type: Schoolhouse
Access: Car
About the Light: *This is the second light in the two-light range at this site. Normally this was the* keeper's quarters as well as the housing for the inner or rear range lamp. This house is located 800 feet inland from the front range.

17 Old Presque Isle

☐ Visited on
_____

Established: 1840
Status: Inactive; museum
Location: (MI) South point of Presque Isle
Type: Conical, rough stone
Access: Car
About the Light: *Driving along US-23, you need to watch closely so as to not pass the sign directing you to the light. Turn toward the lake on Highway 638 and follow to the lighthouse. Although privately owned, this site is open to the public.* Construction of this light took an interesting direction. The bottom part is made of stone and conical in shape, while the top is of brick and round in shape. The lantern room is not the original, but is the lantern room from South Fox Island lighthouse (Lake Michigan) brought to this site as part of a preservation project in the late 1950s.

18 Presque Isle

☐ Visited on
_____

Established: 1870
Status: Active; museum
Location: (MI) Up the road 1 mile from the "Old" light
Type: Conical
Access: Car
About the Light: *Repository of local maritime history would be a good way to describe this site. A collection of fog bells and steam fog whistles as well as maritime artifacts are a part of this location. There is also a nifty gift shop. Erected as a replacement* to the "Old" light, this tower stands 109 feet tall and contains its original Third Order Fresnel optic. It is opened to the public from May to October, and is worth visiting.

19 Forty Mile Point

☐ Visited on

_____

Established: 1896
Status: Active
Location: (MI) On the beach, six miles north of Rogers City
Type: Square/integral brick duplex
Access: Car
About the Light: *Access to this site is easy to miss. After exiting US-23, a sign directs you to the Presque Isle County "Lighthouse Park," but the road leading to the site is not well marked. Do not confuse the road to Forty Mile Point with the road to the Lighthouse Park. Standing 53 feet tall, the structure is constructed of brick and has the keeper's quarters built into it. Half the duplex is being restored as a museum; the other half is the residence for the park manager.*

20 Spectacle Reef

☐ Visited on

_____

Established: 1874
Status: Active
Location: (MI) 12 miles northeast of Cordwood Point in Lake Huron.
Type: Conical, limestone
Access: Boat
About the Light: *Marking a dangerous shoal that is at the bottle-neck of Great Lakes maritime traffic, this light has warned vessels since the mid 1870s. The light was automated in 1972, and is currently solar powered. Spectacle Reef light is often sited as one of the most impressive examples of a monalithal stone lighthouse on the lakes. Its lens was removed in 1982 and is on display at the Great Lakes Historical Society in Vermilion, Ohio.*

21 Poe Reef

☐ Visited on

_____

Established: 1929
Status: Active
Location: (MI) Two and one quarter miles north-west of Cordwood Point in Lake Huron
Type: Square, concrete and steel
Access: Boat
About the Light: *This light is at a point where vessel traffic coming out of Lake Huron is forced to squeeze into the narrow two-mile-wide passage between the Michigan mainland and Bois Blanc Island. Constructed on a 65-foot square cement foundation, the square brick structure stands 60 feet tall. This structure is a near twin to the Martin Reef Light 18 miles to the north, northeast. From 1893 until the building of the light, the site had been marked by a lightship.*

22 Fourteen Foot Shoal

Visited on

☐

Established: 1930
Status: Active
Location: (MI) Just north of Cordwood Point
Type: Round/integral, steel
Access: Boat
About the Light: *No keeper or other staff was ever used at this light. It was radio-controlled from the Poe Reef Light. This, according to the "National Park Service 1994 Inventory of Historic Lighthouses," is said to have been "...an early experiment in off-site operations." Apparently, it worked because no keepers were ever assigned to this facility.*

23 Bois Blanc Island

Visited on

☐

Established: (1829, 1840) 1868
Status: Inactive; private residence
Location: (MI) On the northeast horn of Bois Blanc Island
Type: Square/integral, brick
Access: Boat
About the Light: *The lighthouse is currently a private residence. This point of land, which juts out into Lake Huron like a fang from the island is, even in modern times, an isolated place. The buff-colored lighthouse and its attached keeper's quarters appears to peek through that isolation. For traffic bound from Lake Michigan to Georgian Bay, this spot has always been a danger. Today a 17-foot-tall solar-powered light takes the place of the original lighthouse which was decommissioned in 1955 and sold in 1956. Brick dated 1862 over door refers to date construction began.*

24 Cheboygan Crib Light

Visited on

☐

Established: 1884
Status: Inactive
Location: (MI) Cheboygan River, base of west pier
Type: Octagonal, cast iron
Access: Car
About the Light: *Originally located off shore on a concrete base, it marked the water intake pipe for the city of Cheboygan. Moved to the base of the west pier in 1988, it now lies in a city park.*

25 Cheboygan River Front Range ☐ Visited on

Established: 1880
Status: Active
Location: (MI) West bank of river in city of Cheboygan
Type: Integral, wooden tower and dwelling
Access: Car
About the Light:

26 Old Mackinac Point ☐ Visited on

Established: 1892
Status: Inactive; museum
Location: (MI) By the Mackinac Bridge
Type: Round, brick tower and dwelling
Access: Car
About the Light: *This light is one of the most easily accessed lights in Michigan. Take I-75 to the Mackinac Bridge. The light can be found on the southeast foot of the bridge. Constructed as a fog signal station in 1890, the light was added two years later. In 1957, the Coast Guard deactivated the lighthouse. In 1960, the site became the property of the Mackinac Island State Park Commission and was made into a maritime museum. It is currently the proposed site for a national lighthouse museum.*

27 Round Island ☐ Visited on

Established: 1896
Status: Private aid to navigation
Location: (MI) Straits of Mackinac near Mackinac Island on NW tip of Round Island
Type: Square/integral, brick
Access: Boat
About the Light: *At one time, this was one of the most endangered lights on the lakes. Storms had bitten a full corner out of the keeper's quarters and the elements threatened to wreck the site. Preservation groups stepped in and are currently restoring this light. Although the exterior was restored fully by 1980, work on the inside continues as well as general upkeep. This light was featured in the 1982 movie "Somewhere in Time."*

28 Round Island Passage

☐ Visited on

_____

Established: 1947
Status: Active
Location: (MI) Near breakwater off south shore of Mackinac Island
Type: Hexagonal steel and concrete
Access: Boat
About the Light: *This light is closer to the edge of Round Island Passage than the 1895 light it replaced.*

29 Martin Reef

☐ Visited on

_____

Established: 1927
Status: Active
Location: (MI) Eight and one half miles south of Port Dolomite, in Lake Huron.
Type: Square, concrete and steel
Access: Boat
About the Light: *This light is a near duplicate to the Poe Reef light to the south. The square building is atop a crib and stands 52 feet tall. Due to the remote location of this light, an excursion to visit it would best be done by aircraft or a good-sized boat.*

30 De Tour Reef

☐ Visited on

_____

Established: (1848, 1861) 1931
Status: Active
Location: (MI) Mouth of the St. Marys River.
Type: Square, concrete and steel
Access: Boat
About the Light: *Traffic passing through the locks at Sault Saint Marie use this light as a required reporting point for Soo Control, the Saint Mary's River traffic regulating service. A light was opened at De Tour, on the mainland, in 1848, which is interesting because the locks at the Soo did not open until seven years later. Apparently, traffic in and out of the river was already so heavy that a light was needed. The site was automated in 1974 and continues in activity today. Its original 3-1/2 order lens is on display at DeTour Village Museum.*

31 Shoal Island

☐ Visited on
_____

Established: 1890
Status: Active
Location: (ONT) Off NW tip of St. Joseph Island
Type: Roof-mounted atop wooden dwelling
Access: Boat
About the Light: *Erected atop a lovely two-story building, this light gives the appearance of being little more than decoration. In the 1880s this route was often used by commercial vessels, but today there is absolutely no reason for modern lakeboats to travel this area. The lighthouse is not open to the public.*

32 Wilson Channel Front Range

☐ Visited on
_____

Established: 1905
Status: Active
Location: (ONT) South of Hwy. 17 just east of Hwy 548
Type: Pyramidal, wooden tower
Access: Car
About the Light: *Wilson Channel marks the deep water passage from the St. Marys River in the North Channel above St. Joseph Island. Located at the bottom of a steep hill, this light is the outer or front light in the range. it is constructed of wood and is a near-twin to the inner light. Access to the lights is gained by making a rocky hike along the water which is not recommended.*

33 Wilson Channel Rear Range

☐ Visited on
_____

Established: 1905
Status: Active
Location: (ONT) South of Hwy. 17 just east of Hwy 548
Type: Pyramidal, wooden tower
Access: Car
About the Light: *Wilson Channel marks the deep water passage from the St. Marys River in the North Channel above St. Joseph Island. Located about 600 feet from the front range light, this light is much higher on the hill. From Highway 17, take Highway 548 toward St. Joseph Island and you will find the range to your left just prior to crossing the bridge.*

34 West Sister Rock

☐ Visited on
_____

Established: (1885) 1905
Status: Active
Location: (ONT) Off NE shore of St. Joseph Island
Type: Pyramidal, wooden tower
Access: Boat
About the Light: _Built in 1885 on North Sister Rock and moved to West Sister Rock in 1905, this nondescript lighthouse should be visited by only the most determined light buff. It is located in the far northwestern end of Georgian Bay and is adventurous to access. The light is, however, quite appealing in its simplicity of elegance. It marks the southern edge of the North Channel above St. Joseph Island._

35 McKay Island

☐ Visited on
_____

Established: 1907
Status: Inactive; privately owned
Location: (ONT) Georgian Bay, SE tip of McKay Island, 2 km from Bruce Mines
Type: Roof-mounted on wooden dwelling
Access: Boat
About the Light: _Built to serve the timber industry which had replaced copper mining as the main commercial activity at nearby Bruce Mills, the old light has been replaced with an automated light on a skeleton tower closer to the water._

36 Mississagi Strait

☐ Visited on
_____

Established: 1873
Status: Inactive; museum
Location: (ONT) West end of Manitoulin Island
Type: Pyramidal wooden tower and dwelling
Access: Car
About the Light: _Automated in 1970, this light is another of those terrific Canadian lights that has been given a new life as a museum, this lighthouse once marked the best entrance to the North Channel of Georgian Bay. Beyond this light were the rich Canadian lumber lands and ports such as Blind River and Spanish River. Numbering in the hundreds, wooden lakers with strings of schooner-barges in tow passed this point on their way in and out with their lumber cargoes. Access to this light is gained by driving Highway 540 and exiting at Mississagi Lighthouse Road._

37 Great Duck Island

☐ Visited on

_____

Established: (1877) 1918
Status: Active
Location: (ONT) Southwest side of Great Duck Island, upper Lake Huron
Type: Octagonal reinforced concrete
Access: Boat/helicopter
About the Light: *As an active aid to navigation, this site marks a critical point where lakeboats bound in and out of Georgian Bay make their course change to line up with Cove Island and the mouth of the bay. This is an active station and is not open to public access. It is identical in appearance to the light at Long Point in Lake Erie.*

38 Gore Bay (Janet Head)

☐ Visited on

_____

Established: 1879
Status: Active; private residence
Location: (ONT) End of Water Street, 2 miles NW of Gore Bay
Type: Pyramidal wooden tower and dwelling
Access: Car
About the Light: *Located at the entrance to the Janet Head Campground, this lighthouse is currently used as a private residence. The site is not open to the public. This is a wood structure that is constructed in the Georgian Bay style.*

39 Kagawong

☐ Visited on

_____

Established: (1880, 1888) 1894
Status: Active
Location: (ONT) On hill overlooking Main Street and Harbor
Type: Pyramidal wooden tower
Access: Car
About the Light: *Built to guide ships into a harbor once busy with commercial activity in fishing, timber and paper milling, this is a simple tower containing a modern plastic lamp automated in the early 1960s. Follow Highway 540 into the town of Kagawong and you will find the light near the marina.*

40 Strawberry Island

☐ Visited on

_____

Established: 1881
Status: Active; private residence
Location: (ONT) Northern end of Strawberry Island
Type: Pyramidal wooden tower and dwelling
Access: Boat
About the Light: *This is another in the series of "Georgian Bay style" lighthouses. The structure is wood frame and the light is automated and solar powered. Private owners use the dwelling and it is not open to public access.*

41 Manitowaning

☐ Visited on

_____

Established: 1885
Status: Active
Location: (ONT) On bluff overlooking harbor and village
Type: Pyramidal wooden tower
Access: Car
About the Light: *A wood-framed structure, this light stands 35 feet tall and is still used as an aid to navigation. From Highway 6, take Arthur Road and head toward the bay. The light is at the end of the road and marks the entrance of the once-busy port.*

42 Killarney East

☐ Visited on

_____

Established: (1866) 1909
Status: Active
Location: (ONT) Red Rock Point, 1 mile east of Killarney
Type: Pyramidal wooden tower
Access: Car
About the Light: *Originally dating from 1866 and located on a rough rock out-crop, this simple light was one of the first built to mark the North Channel to assist the fishing and shipping industries and remains active today. Take Highway 637 into Killarney, then follow Ontario Street until it becomes a gravel road. The light is near the end of the road.*

43 Gereaux Island

☐ Visited on

_____

Established: (1870) 1880
Status: Active
Location: (ONT) Mouth of Byng Inlet, northeast Georgian Bay
Type: Pyramidal wooden tower
Access: Boat
About the Light: *This appears to have been the first of the "Georgian Bay" style lights with a wood-framed pyramidal two- or three-story tower with attached single-story keeper's quarters and rear slanted utility room. There are six of these structures in this area and they are almost identical in appearance in Canadian waters and were constructed between 1870 and 1889. The Gereaux Island light is a 48-foot-tall wood-framed structure and is erected on what is little more than a small rock out-crop laced with some pine trees. Automated in 1989, this is a season rescue station and visitors are welcome.*

44 Byng Inlet Range

☐ Visited on

_____

Established: 1890
Status: Active
Location: (ONT) Byng Inlet, close to the south side of the channel
Type: Pyramidal wooden tower
Access: Boat
About the Light: *This range marks the correct approach into the mouth of Byng Inlet, clear of the Magnetawan Ledges and Burton Bank. Both this light and the rear range (not pictured) were tended by the Gereaux Island keeper.*

45 Pointe au Baril

☐ Visited on

_____

Established: 1889
Status: Active
Location: (ONT) Pointe au Baril
Type: Pyramidal wooden tower and dwelling
Access: Boat
About the Light: *Unlike many of the ports in Georgian Bay, Pointe au Baril is best known for tourism, rather than the shipping of lumber or grain products. This light is of the Georgian Bay style. One reason the lights look alike is that many were contracted to the same few people to construct them. Wood-framed, it stands just over two stories tall and has an attached keeper's quarters.*

46 Red Rock

☐ Visited on

_____

Established: (1870, 1881) 1911
Status: Active
Location: (ONT) Red Rock Island at entrance to
Parry Sound
Type: Elliptical, reinforced concrete
Access: Boat
About the Light: *This light is little more than a heli-pad stuck atop a rock that juts above the water. Between the pad and the tower, a navigation light has been sandwiched. You would have to be a true, first-class lighthouse nut to want to visit this remote site. The helipad was added in the early 1970s to provide easier access.*

47 Snug Harbour

☐ Visited on

_____

Established: 1894
Status: Active
Location: (ONT) South end of Snug Island; north side of harbour entrance
Type: Pyramidal/integral
Access: Boat
About the Light: *Located between the peninsula that creates Snug Harbour and Franklyn Island, this isolated lighthouse is actually part of a range. To get to the light, drive down Highway 559 to Snug Harbour Road and follow that road to the marina at the end. Then tell every boater that you are the transcendent being of lighthouses and must get out to see the light at any cost. One of them may then take pity on you and boat you out to look at the light close up. Swimming is not recommended.*

48 Jones Island

☐ Visited on

_____

Established: 1894
Status: Active
Location: (ONT) Jones Island near Parry Sound
Type: Roof-mounted tower on wooden dwelling
Access: Boat
About the Light: *Looking like a cardboard cut-out set upon the rocks, this is another of the Georgian Bay's range lights. This particular range light guides vessels into Parry Sound. The wood-framed light itself is 50 feet tall, but sits substantially higher on top of the rocks of the island. The site is accessible only by boat.*

49 Western Island

☐ Visited on

Established: 1895
Status: Active
Location: (ONT) 22 mi. SW of Parry Sound, on Double Top Island, the south group of the Western Islands
Type: Octagonal wooden tower
Access: Boat
About the Light: *Apparently inappropriately named, there seems to be nothing "western" about the island cluster on which this light is erected. The fact is that the rock out-crops of this cluster are in the southeast part of Georgian Bay, and the only reasoning for calling this light the "Western Island light" is the fact that it sits upon the western-most rock in the cluster. Perhaps the chain then gained its name from the light rather than the other way around. The tower stands 60 feet tall.*

50 Brebeuf Island

☐ Visited on

Established: (1878) 1900
Status: Active; private cottage
Location: (ONT) North end of Brebeuf Island
Type: Pyramidal wooden tower and dwelling
Access: Boat
About the Light: *Originally built on Gin Rock in 1878, the light was moved to Brebeuf in 1900 to form a front range light with the rear light on Beausoleil Island. This range leads to Penetang, Midland, Victoria Harbour and Port Severn in southeastern Georgian Bay.*

51 Beausoleil Island

☐ Visited on

Established: (1900) 1915
Status: Active
Location: (ONT) West shore of Brebeuf Island
Type: Skeletal with enclosed lantern and top
Access: Boat
About the Light: *This is the rear range light of a range formed with Brebeuf Island light as the front light.*

52 Hope Island

☐ Visited on
_____

Established: 1884
Status: Inactive, ruins
Location: (ONT) Northeast tip of Hope Island
Type: Pyramidal wooden tower and attached dwelling
Access: Boat
About the Light: _Once again that common construction form used in so many Georgian Bay style lighthouses is seen here. The light is atop a wood-framed, two-story tower with a keeper's quarters attached. Hope Island is located at the entrance to the narrow passage leading through the shoal-studded route to Midland, Ontario. It is appropriately named, because many a mariner has approached this area in the hope of sighting this light. In 1911, the crew of the THOMAS CRANAGE apparently missed this landmark and ended up wrecking the largest wooden steamer in the world._

53 Christian Island

☐ Visited on
_____

Established: 1859
Status: Active
Location: (ONT) Southern "horn" of Christian Island
Type: Conical; limestone imperial tower (1 of 6)
Access: Boat
About the Light: _Back in 1859 when this light was commissioned, this part of Georgian Bay was a heavily traveled area. Today, there is far less shipping activity in the area. The light is now automated with a plastic beacon where its once-elegant lantern room was erected. Constructed of rough stone blocks the light stands next to the ruins of the former keeper's quarters. Access is gained by taking the ferry over from the town of Cedar Point._

54 Nottawasaga Island

☐ Visited on
_____

Established: 1858
Status: Active
Location: (ONT) Southwest coast of Nottawasaga Island
Type: Conical; limestone imperial tower (1 of 6)
Access: Boat
About the Light: _Marking the approach to the bustling port city of Collingwood, Ontario, this light was constructed upon an island two and one half miles out of that port. The light stands just over 80 feet tall and is constructed of limestone. As the 1960 season opened, the light, having been automated the previous season, no longer needed a keeper. Considering the light's distance from shore, it is best visited by boat._

55 Griffith Island

☐ Visited on

_____

Established: 1858
Status: Active
Location: (ONT) On the northwest shore of Griffith Island
Type: Conical; limestone imperial tower (1 of 6)
Access: Boat
About the Light: *Griffith Island is one of three islands that block the entrance to Colopys Bay and the port of Wiarton, Ontario. Hay Island and White Cloud Island make up the other two. The tower of this rough block lighthouse stands 80 feet tall and is in good condition when compared to the nearby keeper's quarters which are abandoned. This light is on the outside of the island and a good distance from the mainland it is not easily visited, so use of a boat or aircraft may be needed.*

56 Cape Croker

☐ Visited on

_____

Established: (1898) 1909
Status: Active
Location: (ONT) NE end of Cape Croker
Type: Octagonal reinforced concrete
Access: Car
About the Light: *Standing 53 feet tall, the tower contains a modern airport-style rotating beacon. The light was originally built to aid navigation around the Bruce Peninsula. The road to the light passes through Chippewas of Nawash First Nation community before narrowing to one lane, 4.5 miles long.*

57 Lion's Head

☐ Visited on

_____

Established: (1903, 1911) 1983
Status: Inactive
Location: (ONT) Village waterfront
Type: Pyramidal wooden tower
Access: Car
About the Light: *During the "Great Storm of 1913," which wrecked more than a dozen giant lakeboats and killed more than 250 mariners, the original light built in 1911 at this site was said to have been swept into the bay. This light was constructed as its replacement. In 1967, the light was deactivated and in 1969, demolished. In 1983, design students at Bruce Peninsula District School constructed this replica. From Highway 6, take County Road 9 into Lion's Head and weave through town toward the bay. The light is in a small park that is bay-side.*

58 Cabot Head

Visited on

Established: 1896
Status: Inactive; museum
Location: (ONT) Cabot Head Point on the northeast tip of the Bruce Peninsula.
Type: Square/integral wood tower and dwelling
Access: Car
About the Light: *A steel airport-style light erected in 1971 has replaced the old light tower. The remaining building, however, has been turned into a museum. The light tower, which had been removed in 1971, was rebuilt in 1995 as part of a restoration program. To get to this light, take Highway 6 until you nearly drop off the world. Then turn off on Dyer's Bay Road and follow that six miles to the light.*

59 Flowerpot Island

Visited on

Established: (1897) 1968
Status: Active
Location: (ONT) NE tip of Flowerpot Island
Type: Skeletal
Access: Boat
About the Light: *The 1987 lighthouse was built to guide traffic through the treacherous Tobermory Islands. Regrettably, the old wooden light was torn down in 1969, the year after this new steel skeleton tower was put into service. Flowerpot Island, now a part of Fathom Five National Marine Park, is open to the public.*

60 Lonely Island

Visited on

Established: (1870) 1907
Status: Active
Location: (ONT) On summit of North Bluff
Type: Octagonal wooden tower
Access: Boat
About the Light: *Living up to its name this light is in one of the most remote parts of the Great Lakes. Standing just over 50 feet tall, the wood frame light is now automated and solar powered. Access is by boat, and since this is an operational aid to navigation it is not open to the public.*

61 South Baymouth Front Range

Established: 1898
Status: Active
Location: (ONT) North side of Baymouth
Type: Pyramidal wooden tower
Access: Car
About the Light: *Once a busy fishing village, ferries and tourists are now the businesses of South BayMouth. A modern car ferry running between South Baymouth and Tobermory now links Manitoulin Island to the Bruce Peninsula. Part of a set of near twin ranges, this light is the outer of the site. To get to the range, take Highway 6 downbound until you reach the lake; look to your right and you will see the light.*

62 South Baymouth Rear Range

Established: 1898
Status: Active
Location: (ONT) 783 feet behind the front light
Type: Pyramidal wooden tower
Access: Car
About the Light: *This is the inner light of the range. Its wood-framed structure is nearly identical to that of the outer light. The inner light is inland from its sister light.*

63 Cove Island

Established: 1858
Status: Active
Location: (ONT) NW tip of Cove Island.
Type: Conical, limestone imperial tower (1 of 6)
Access: Boat
About the Light: *One of the true sentinels of the Great Lakes, this 80-foot-tall gleaming white monolith is as important to mariners today as it was in 1858 when it was built. Cove Island marks the entrance to mighty Georgian Bay. The safe passage for vessels in and out of the bay and past Cove Island and its nearby shoals is just over 6000 feet wide. Some mariners found the passage; some found their doom. Among the dozens of wrecks in this area is thought to be the first sailing ship on the lakes, THE GRIFFON, lost on its first voyage in 1679. This has always been a dangerous place.*

64 Big Tub

☐ Visited on

_____

Established: (1881) 1885
Status: Active
Location: (ONT) Lighthouse Point on Big Tub Harbour, west entrance to Tobermory
Type: Hexagonal wooden tower
Access: Car

About the Light: *Standing on a small shelf of rock, this 44-foot-tall light faces Georgian Bay without much protection. Its six-sided wooden tower must have been constructed of the finest Canadian lumber because so far it has been more than a match for the bay's temper. Following Highway 6 into Tobermory, you can take Front Street, which curves around toward the lighthouse. The site itself is concealed by high trees until you get right up to it. A car ferry now links Tobermory to South Baymouth on Manitoulin Island.*

65 Chantry Island

☐ Visited on

_____

Established: 1859
Status: Active
Location: (ONT) Just west of Southhampton on east shore of island
Type: Conical, limestone imperial tower (1 of 6)
Access: Boat

About the Light: *Although the keeper's quarters are nothing but ruins, the light still stands proudly. The island itself is not far off the mainland, so by driving along Highway 21 and exiting on Claredon Road just prior to the river you can double back along the shore. The light can be seen from the mainland.*

66 Saugeen River Front Range

☐ Visited on

_____

Established: 1883
Status: Active
Location: (ONT) west end of north pier
Type: Pyramidal wooden tower
Access: Car, foot

About the Light: *This is the outer-most of the twin range-light towers guiding ships into the Saugeen River and the town of Southampton. Located on a pier that extends nearly 100 feet into the lake, the wooden tower stands a bit more than 30 feet tall. To get to this tower, take Highway 21 north through South Hampton and across the Saugeen River. Turn left on Rankin Street and proceed on foot.*

67 Saugeen River Rear Range

Established: 1903
Status: Active
Location: (ONT) South Rankin Street just east of Hwy 21
Type: Pyramidal wooden tower
Access: Car
About the Light: *This is the rear light of a range guiding ships into the Saugeen River and the town of Southampton. The access to this light is, oddly, in the other direction of that of the front range. This light is farther inland and so you must exit Highway 21 to the right on Rankin Street. The light is just past that turn.*

68 Kincardine

Established: 1881
Status: Active
Location: (ONT) North bank of the Penetagore River
Type: Octagonal wooden tower
Access: Car
About the Light: *One of the most historic harbors on Lake Huron, this port has a legacy that goes back way beyond this light. The wood-framed lighthouse is actually part of a range and is constructed atop the keeper's quarters. The light looks out over a shoreline that is studded with wooden shipwrecks buried in the sands. Take Kincardine Ave. into town and you can not miss the light. It is on the southwest corner of Harbour Street and Huron Terrace Street.*

69 Point Clark

Established: 1859
Status: Active
Location: (ONT) Nine miles south of Kincardine
Type: Conical, limestone imperial tower (1 of 6)
Access: Car
About the Light: *Standing 80 feet tall, this rough stone block structure is a true classic. This light was proclaimed a Canadian National Historic Sight and today supports a maritime museum during the summer months. Getting there is easy; just take Highway 21 and get off at Huron Concession #2. Take that to Huron Road and turn right at Lighthouse Road.*

70 Goderich

☐ Visited on

_____

Established: 1847
Status: Active
Location: (ONT) South of Goderich Harbor at end of Lighthouse Street
Type: Square masonry tower
Access: Car

About the Light: *One of the earliest lights on Lake Huron, the Goderich Main light was constructed up on a bluff overlooking the lake. For that reason, the light needed to be only 35 feet tall. This "blockhouse" style of construction appears as if it will stand for many decades to come. To get there follow Highway 21 to the city of Goderich and exit on either Hamilton, Kingston or East streets. In a short distance you will come to a "roundabout" follow it to West Street and follow that to the light.*

WHAT MADE THE TAWAS POINT LIGHT WINK?

Often, when looking across history, the little details are lost. The question always seems to come up, "How exactly did they do that?" For example, when considering lighthouses of the past, we know that the source of light used was the flame from a lamp that was normally oil fed. Some lights, however were said to flash at given intervals so that they could be better identified against the other lights ashore. But, when you look at an oil lamp, the question comes to mind: *how do you make it blink without putting out the flame?*

Luck has it that the method used for making some of the lights blink has been left in detail for us to discover. The problem is that the information has been hidden away for more than a century in the *"Annual Reports of the Activity of the Lighthouse Board"* to which few in the public have access. The method, however, is so simple as to be as brilliant as the lights themselves. It was formally named "The Occulting Light."

It is important to keep in mind that in the early 1890s there were no compact electric motors or electronic controls to make a lighthouse blink. Additionally, most lighthouses were located in isolated areas where a small staff had to tend to all of the workings. Bulky and complex equipment were not practical for operations in these areas. For that reason, the known technology had to be used, and an easy-to-maintain device needed to be developed. Problems were encountered in the use of wheels and rollers that were used to rotate shields past the lamps. Although the lights appeared to blink, the equipment required constant lubrication and tended to wear out rapidly. Additionally, the rate of rotation was no higher than one rotation every four minutes. A method using a shaded lens floated upon a pool of mercury was tried and the rotation rate was increased to one rotation every 30 seconds. Called the Mahan system, after its

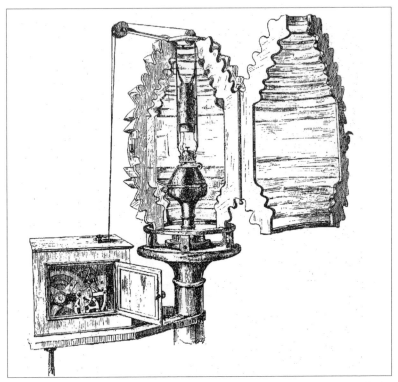

Seen here in use on a "Funck-type" lamp, the occulting clock was what made the Tawas light wink...

– Annual Report of the Activity of the Lighthouse Board, 1894.

designer Captain F.A. Mahan of the Army Corps of Engineers, this equipment was nasty to install and maintain and was only tried in a few lights on the east coast. In some lights, the whole lens was rotated with "flash panels" being constructed into the lens itself.

Another problem came from the light source itself. Simple oil lamps were burned to create the light which was then refracted through hand-crafted lenses and formed into a powerful beam. These lamps needed fuel and had to be fed with combustible oil, and also needed to be vented so that their heat and smoke could be released. For that reason, tall glass chimneys were used on many lamps of the Great Lakes. This nearly universal source of power did not lend itself well to high speed rotation.

All of this led to the Lighthouse Board searching for a more simple method to make their lights wink. The problem was resolved by the use of the most common mechanism of the day: clock-work. It was called the occulting clock mechanism and here is how it worked. A clock-work system of springs and gears was constructed so that rather than moving the hands of a clock-face, they would simply throw a rocker

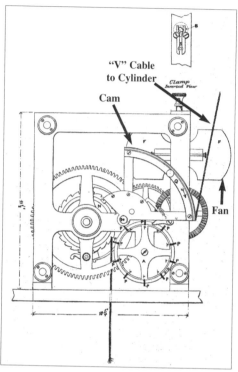

Detailed view of occulting clock.

cam. To the cam was attached thin "V" shaped cable that was run up through two pulleys and whose other end was attached to a brass cylinder. That cylinder was attached to two tracks that ran up and down along the sides of the lamp chimney. When the cam drove up, it allowed the cable to slack and the brass cylinder to drop over the lamp blocking the light from the wick. A moment later the cam drove down pulling the cylinder up and allowing the light to show. The process was repeated at high rates of speed giving the light the ability to flash on and off at whatever frequency and intervals that the clockwork was set. Very narrow limits could be set into this simple machine, thus giving each light its own signature. Additionally, the fans within the clockwork could be adjusted to give even greater identity to the light. Each day, the lightkeeper had to wind the

Occulting clock mechanism so that it would be ready for the night's operation. In such cases a large hand-crank was used. The whole device was an expense of $1,000 including the installation.

Convinced that the occulting light was one of the neatest ideas in lighthouse operation, the Lighthouse Board proceeded to equip several stations with the device. One of the first seven lights in the nation to get the new contraption was the lighthouse at Tawas Point, Michigan. The device worked quite well and was later added to other stations. Today, the light at Tawas still flashes, but the wonders of electricity are doing the job. As of this writing, the light is slated for deactivation, but the flashing of the current optic serves to remind us of the little details of how things worked more than a century ago. Now you know exactly what made the Tawas Point lighthouse wink.

THE
LIGHTS
OF LAKE
MICHIGAN

GREAT LAKES LIGHTHOUSES

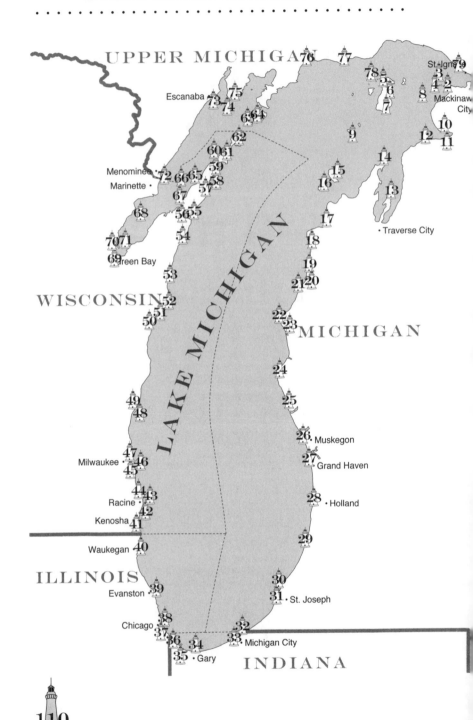

UPPER MICHIGAN

76
77
St Ignace 79
78
3
5
4 2
Escanaba 73 75
74
6
7
Mackinaw
City

63 64
62
9
10
60 51
59
14
12
58
15
11
Menominee 72 66 65
16
Marinette 57
67
13
68 56 55
17
Traverse City
54
18
70 71
19
69 Green Bay
21 20
53

WISCONSIN 52
22
51
23 MICHIGAN
50
24

25

49
48
26 Muskegon

27 Grand Haven
47
46
Milwaukee 45
28 Holland
44 43
Racine 42
Kenosha 41
29

Waukegan 40

ILLINOIS
30
Evanston 39
31 St. Joseph

38
37
32
36 34
33 Michigan City
35 Gary
INDIANA

LAKE MICHIGAN

110

The Lights of Lake Michigan

1 McGulpin Point
2 Waugoshance
3 White Shoal
4 Grays Reef Light
5 Squaw Island
6 St. James Harbor
7 Beaver Island
8 Ile Aux Galets (Skillagalee)
9 South Fox Island
10 Little Traverse (Harbor Point)
11 Petoskey Pierhead
12 Charlevoix South Pierhead
13 Old Mission
14 Grand Traverse
15 North Manitou Shoal
16 South Manitou Island
17 Manning Memorial Lighthouse
18 Point Betsie
19 Frankfort North Breakwater
20 Manistee North Pierhead
21 Old Manistee Main
22 Big Sable
23 Ludington North Pierhead
24 Little Sable
25 White River
26 Muskegon South Pierhead
27 Grand Haven

28 Holland
29 South Haven
30 St. Joseph North Pier
31 St. Joseph Lighthouse Depot
32 Old Michigan City
33 Michigan City East Pier
34 Gary Breakwater
35 Buffington Breakwater
36 Indiana Harbor East Breakwater
37 Chicago Harbor
38 Chicago Harbor Southeast Guidewall
39 Grosse Point
40 Waukegan Harbor (Little Fort)
41 Kenosha Lighthouse (Southport)
42 Kenosha North Pier
43 Racine North Breakwater
44 Wind Point
45 Milwaukee Pierhead
46 Milwaukee Breakwater
47 North Point
48 Port Washington Breakwater
49 Old Port Washington Light
50 Manitowoc
51 Two Rivers North Pierhead
52 Two Rivers Point (Rawley Point)

53 Kewaunee Pierhead
54 Algoma Pierhead
55 Sturgeon Bay Ship Canal
56 Sturgeon Bay Ship Canal North Pierhead
57 Old Bailey's Harbor
58 Bailey's Harbor Range
59 Cana Island
60 Plum Island
61 Pilot Island (Port des Mort Passage)
62 Pottawatomie
63 St. Martin Island
64 Poverty Island
65 Eagle Bluff
66 Chambers Island
67 Sherwood Point
68 Peshtigo Reef
69 Green Bay Harbor Entrance
70 Grassy Island Front Range
71 Longtail Point (Ruins)
72 Menominee North Pier
73 Sand Point
74 Minneapolis Shoal
75 Peninsula Point
76 Manistique East Breakwater
77 Seul Choix Point
78 Lansing Shoal
79 St. Helena

117

Lake Michigan

Most accounts give the discovery of Lake Michigan to Jean Nicolet in 1634. But, when Nicolet reached the land of the Paunts, or "Stinkers," he would be nothing more than the first white man to visit the region. The people here were said to come from the place of "paunt" water or "Stinking Water" which meant salt water. They were said to have come from the north paunt waters, perhaps Hudson Bay, and migrated to the Great Lakes. Nicolet had already been forewarned by the people of the Huron Tribe that this distant lake was a place where the Paunts lived, but the French explorer thought that he knew better than his Huron guides. So, certain that the Huron's meant that the people of China were actually the Paunts, Nicolet departed Quebec City armed with a bright Chinese robe. In some circles it is thought that Nicolet's journey actually went up to Lake Superior, while other schools of thought say that he went to Lake Michigan. There is no written account of this trip, but the fact remains that if the explorer clad in a Chinese robe went in any direction of discovery on the new lake he would have found that the people of the "Winnebagoe," "Algonkin" or the "Ojibwa" tribes had beaten him to the discovery by quite a few centuries. Without regard to which lake he actually went, Nicolet must have looked a sight as he greeted the expected Mandarins with his authentic robe and got fed beaver meat rather than Chinese noodles.

Lake Michigan is the only one of the five Great Lakes that does not have a Canadian shore. It is instead surrounded by the states of Michigan, Indiana, Illinois and Wisconsin. Considering that Chicago was probably being settled before the white man even knew that Lake Erie existed, we can see the potential for marine traffic across Lake Michigan. Measuring 80 miles across at its widest point and more than 350 miles long, Lake Michigan can hold her own with the rest of the lakes in size. This lake can also hold her own in the numbers of ship-wrecks that she contains. Lake Michigan is responsible for almost 800 ship-wrecks, or 21 percent of all of the Great Lakes shipwrecks. This is second only to Lake Huron.

Some of the most interesting lighthouses ever constructed on the lakes are found along the shores of Lake Michigan. As with all of the lakes, some of these sites have fallen into despair while others have been lovingly restored. Oddly, this lake is the site of many "red" lighthouses. As if colored to tell the mariner that they are in fact on Lake Michigan, many of the lighthouses are simply painted pure red. None of the other lakes have pure red lighthouses. Also this lake is the home of the only "candy-stripe" lighthouse on the great lakes. The reason for this phenomena in paint schemes is unknown at this time to this author.

From top to bottom, the Michigan shore of the lake has become the "Gold Coast" of the Great Lakes. Expensive cottages line the beaches and harbors such as South Haven, Holland and Grand Traverse are the repository of expensive yachts. Towns such as Suttons Bay – were once just out-of-the-way fishing vil-lages – are now the haven of up-scale shops, shoppers and restaurants. Cash-flow lost in the crash of the auto industry is being regained a little at a time in the tourist industry. Year round, Lake Michigan's Gold Coast thrives.

1 McGulpin Point

☐ Visited on

Established: 1869
Status: Inactive; private residence
Location: (MI) 3 miles west of Mackinaw City
Type: Octagonal/integral brick tower and dwelling
Access: Car
About the Light: *The lantern room was removed from this site, and it is now a private residence. This structure is made of brick and the octagonal tower is integral to the residence. The light was deactivated in 1906 and replaced by the Old Mackinac Point light.*

2 Waugoshance

☐ Visited on

Established: (1832 Lightship) 1851
Status: Inactive; ruins
Location: (MI) 17 miles west of the Mackinac Bridge
Type: Conical brick tower
Access: Boat
About the Light: *Deactivated in 1910 and abandoned in 1912, this light was said to have been made "obsolete" by the building of the White Shoal light, and was later used as a World War II bombing target. It retains one of only three "bird-cage" style lantern rooms left on the lakes. At one time it had an iron skirt that wrapped around the stone tower. That skirt has since come loose and dropped into the lake. This is one of the most endangered lighthouses on the Great Lakes. SEE STORY ON PAGE 143.*

3 White Shoal

☐ Visited on

Established: (1891 Lightship) 1910
Status: Active
Location: (MI) 20 miles west of Mackinac Bridge
Type: Conical, steel and concrete
Access: Boat
About the Light: *This is the only "candy cane" striped lighthouse on the Great Lakes. Its giant red and white markings can be recognized from many miles away. This tower was erected in 1910 to replace the lightship, and made the Waugoshance light obsolete, thus giving that stations crew a chance to vacate and escape the ghost of John Herman. In 1976 the light was automated. The tower itself stands 121 feet tall. The light is not open to public access. The Second Order lens was removed in 1984 and is on display at Whitefish Point Ship* .eck *Museum.*

4 Grays Reef Light

☐ Visited on
_____

Established: (1891 Lightship) 1936
Status: Active
Location: (MI) 24 miles west of the Mackinac Bridge
Type: "Arts Decoratifs," or art deco; steel and concrete
Access: Boat
About the Light: _Constructed in 1936, this modern light station has the art deco look of the 30s. Made of steel, it was a replacement for the series of lightships that stood on guard at this position over the years. Lightships Number 57, 56 and 99 had all taken their turn in this position prior to the placement of this structure. In 1976, this light was automated and remains in service today._

5 Squaw Island

☐ Visited on
_____

Established: 1892
Status: Inactive; stabilized ruins
Location: (MI) Beaver Island chain, 42 miles west of the Mackinac Bridge
Type: Octagonal/integral red brick tower and dwelling
Access: Boat
About the Light: _Standing abandoned, the only thing that has kept this light from being vandalized is its remote location in northern Lake Michigan. The nearest point of mainland is an isolated shore of Michigan's Upper Peninsula 11 miles to the north. The site itself consists of a stylish brick tower and attached keeper's quarters. These are treacherous waters and accessing the light is not advised._

6 St. James Harbor

☐ Visited on
_____

Established: (1856) 1870
Status: Active
Location: (MI) Whiskey Point, NE edge of harbor
Type: Conical, brick
Access: Carferry
About the Light: _This brick tower stands 41 feet tall and has a focal plane of 38 feet. Located on Beaver Island, the light was established to enable mariners to use this harbor as a refuge from severe weather in northern Lake Michigan and is accessible by way of ferry boat from the Michigan mainland. The dwelling was demolished in 1956. Currently, the light is an active aid to navigation, but you can walk near it and get good photos._

7 Beaver Island (Beaver Head)
☐ Visited on

Established: (1852) 1858
Status: Inactive
Location: (MI) South end of Beaver Island
Type: Conical, brick tower and attached dwelling
Access: Car/Ferry
About the Light: *You can access this light by catching the ferry over to Beaver Island. The structure is made of brick and is used today as an environmental education facility by the Charlevoix Public Schools. The house was built in 1866. Its use as a light came to an end in 1962. The site is open to the public.*

8 Ile Aux Galets (Skillagalee)
☐ Visited on

Established: (1850, 1868) 1888
Status: Active
Location: (MI) East of shipping channel, SW of Waugoshance
Type: Octagonal brick tower
Access: Boat
About the Light: *The name means "island of pebbles." This light stands alone like a pillar and is one of the best-looking lighthouses on Lake Michigan. The tower is identical to that at Port Sanilac. The Light Station once occupied the entire island, but its dwelling and outbuildings were demolished in 1969. Its Fourth Order Fresnel lens has been replaced by a 300mm plastic lens and the light is automated. This is an active aid to navigation and is not open to the public.*

9 South Fox Island
☐ Visited on

Established: (1868) 1934
Status: Inactive
Location: (MI) Southern tip of South Fox Island, 26 miles west of Charlevoix.
Type: Square/integral brick tower and dwelling
Access: Boat
About the Light :*Actually this is the site of two lights. Made of brick, the original tower and attached keeper's quarters are boarded up and abandoned, but in fair condition. Closer to the beach a 60-foot-tall steel tower stands with a nearby keeper's house. All of these structures are abandoned. An old lantern room from South Fox Island was transported to Old Presque Isle Light (1840) on Lake Huron in 1959 for installation there as part of its restoration.*

10 Little Traverse

☐ Visited on

_____

Established: 1884
Status: Inactive; private residence
Location: (MI) Southern tip of Harbor Point
Type: Square
Access: Restricted

About the Light: *Property on which this light resides is very private and both guards and gates will stop anyone from accessing the site. The light's first keeper was one of the famed "Ladies of the lakes," Mrs. Elizabeth Whitney Williams. Previous to being* assigned as keeper of this light in 1884, Elizabeth had been the keeper of the Beaver Island light. That position was assigned to her after her husband, who was the keeper prior to her, had been drowned while attempting to rescue the crew of the distressed schooner THOMAS H. HOWLAND.

Fog Signal Bell for Little Traverse Light

☐ Visited on

_____

Established: 1884
Status: Inactive
Location: (MI) In front of the lighthouse
Type: Pyramidal wood-framed belfry
Access: Restricted as above

About the Light: *A very rare example of a fog signal bell that has survived into the present. Note the modern skeletal light tower in the background, which replaced the lighthouse in 1961.*

11 Petoskey Pierhead

☐ Visited on

_____

Established: Modern structure
Status: Active
Location: (MI) End of west pier
Type: Cylindrical steel and concrete
Access: Car

About the Light: *Replaced earlier lights dating from the late 1880s and early 1990s.*

12 Charlevoix South Pierhead

☐ Visited on

_____

Established: (1885) 1948
Status: Active
Location: (MI) West end of south pier
Type: Pyramidal steel on skeletal base
Access: Car
About the Light: *The first pier light of 1885 was a square wooden structure located on the north pier and was subsequently moved to the south pier in 1914, then replaced by the current light. Charlevoix is a tourist Mecca.*

13 Old Mission

☐ Visited on

_____

Established: 1870
Status: Inactive; private residence
Location: (MI) Northern tip of old Mission Point, Grand Traverse Bay
Type: Square/integral wooden tower and dwelling
Access: Car
About the Light: *Driving north on Michigan Route 37 to its end, you will find the light. This light is attached to a wood-framed structure and now is also part of a local park. The tower stands 30 feet tall, but its optic has been removed. In 1933 the site was deactivated and was then taken over by the state. Currently, Peninsula Township owns the site and although the building is not open to the public, the grounds are accessible. Mission Point Light is located on the 45th parallel of latitude, halfway between the equator and north pole.*

14 Grand Traverse

☐ Visited on

_____

Established: (1853) 1958
Status: Inactive; museum
Location: (MI) Cat's Head Point, Leelanau State Park
Type: Square/integral roof-mounted lantern on brick dwelling
Access: Car
About the Light: *Taking Michigan Route 22 north to M-201, and that road to County Road 640, you can access County Road 629 which leads to the state park and the light. The light itself consists of a tower atop a two and one half-story brick building. Currently the restored light is a museum and gift shop and well worth the drive required to get there. An automatic light was built nearby in 1972.*

15 North Manitou Shoal

☐ Visited on
_____

Established: 1935
Status: Active
Location: (MI) Halfway between North Manitou Island and Pyramid Point, due east of Leland
Type: Square
Access: Boat
About the Light: *This site looks a lot like Alcatraz. Although the lantern room itself has some artistic appeal with diamond glass panels winding gracefully around it, the rest of the light is not much to look upon. The structure is made of steel and concrete and was automated in 1980. The light is 60 feet tall and is not open to the public. This structure replaced a lightship that had been stationed here since 1910.*

16 South Manitou Island ☐ Visited on
_____

Established: (1839, 1858) 1872
Status: Inactive
Location: (MI) Southeast tip of South Manitou Island
Type: Conical brick tower
Access: Boat
About the Light: *In stark contrast to the Manitou Shoal light, this light is an eye-pleasing and photogenic sight. Although the original light was established here in 1839, the current 100-foot-tall light replaced the old light in 1872. Ferry service from the town of Leland, Michigan, will allow you to access this sight as well as other interesting aspects of the island. The light and the island are under the management of the National Park Service and are part of the Sleeping Bear Dunes National Lakeshore.*

17 Manning Memorial Lighthouse

☐ Visited on
_____

Established: 1991
Status: Active
Location: (MI) Empire, Michigan public beach
Type: Cylindrical wood and stucco memorial
Access: Car
About the Light: *This light is only a "lighthouse" in the artistic sense. The site was constructed and illuminated to honor Mr. Robert H. Manning, a long-time resident of the city of Empire. Mr. Manning had always wished for a light to help guide him in off the lake after his fishing trips. The light and surrounding park honors his wish, yet serves no other use as a navigation aid. The park is open to the public.*

18 Point Betsie

Established: 1858
Status: Active
Location: (MI) Five miles north of Frankfort
Type: Round/integral brick tower and dwelling
Access: Car
About the Light: *Standing only 37 feet tall, this brick tower is painted white and has been in service since 1858. You can see the station by taking Michigan Route 22 along the coast and exiting at Point Betsie Road. One of the last lights to be automated (in 1983) it continued to serve as a Coast Guard residence until the winter of 1996 when the boiler failed, forcing the families to vacate due to lack of heat. In February 1996, the rotating mechanism for the Fresnel lens failed and the lens was removed and put on display at the Sleeping Bear Dunes Maritime Museum.*

19 Frankfort North Breakwater

☐ Visited on

Established: (1873) 1932
Status: Active
Location: (MI) End of north breakwater
Type: Pyramidal, square steel tower
Access: Car
About the Light: *An active aid to navigation, this 67-foot-tower is a simple steel constructed box connected to the mainland by an elevated catwalk. The pier on which it is mounted is a treacherous place with seas always sweeping it, so walking out to the light is not recommended. Driving up M-22 to Frankfort and Main Street will take you to the shore from where the light can been seen.*

20 Manistee North Pierhead

☐ Visited on

Established: (1873) 1927
Status: Active
Location: (MI) On the end of the north Pierhead, Manistee, Michigan
Type: Conical, steel
Access: Car
About the Light: *Constructed on the end of the Manistee pierhead, this light was accessed by the keepers by way of an elevated catwalk. Over the years the original catwalk, which was made of wood, was often battered by the weather and later repaired. Today a modern catwalk is in place with a lot of steel and wire. No doubt that the lake will one day do its worst on this structure as well. The tower of the light itself is made of steel bands and standing 39 feet tall, appears to be more than a match for Lake Michigan.*

21 Old Manistee Main

☐ Visited on

Established: 1870
Status: Inactive; private residence
Location: (MI) 3 blocks from 5th Avenue Beach Park
Type: Square/integral wooden tower and dwelling
Access: Car
About the Light: *The roof-mounted lantern and cupola were removed long ago. This building has been moved several times since it was deactivated around 1927. Serving for a long time as a rental property, it has recently undergone extensive renovation as a private home.*

22 Big Sable

☐ Visited on

Established: 1867
Status: Active
Location: (MI) Eight and one half miles north of Ludington
Type: Conical, brick tower sheathed in cast-iron plates
Access: Foot (1.5 mile hike from campground)
About the Light: *Stunning is the best way to describe this black and white iron-plated monster. Standing 112 feet tall, it dominates the lakeshore. Automated in 1968, it is protected by being a part of the Ludington State Park. In the late 1970s, this light was about to be undermined by the waves, and the "D-9" pole light was constructed to take its place. The Big Sable Lighthouse Keeper's Association stepped in and saved the light. Ironically, the new light now cannot go into service because the functioning and historic original light blocks it out. Its Third Order lens is on display in Ludington.*

23 Ludington North Pierhead

☐ Visited on

Established: (1871) 1924
Status: Active
Location: (MI) North Pierhead
Type: Pyramidal, steel and concrete
Access: Car
About the Light: *This light is odd in the shape of the structure's foundation. Shaped much like the bow of a large ship, the base of the structure was constructed to fight off the waves and ice. The tower itself is made of riveted steel plates. Access to the site is gained by simply walking out onto the breakwall which was rebuilt and squared off in 1994 in front of the light.*

24 Little Sable

☐ Visited on

_____

Established: 1874
Status: Active
Location: (MI) Ten miles south of Pentwater, Michigan
Type: Conical brick
Access: Car
About the Light: *One of the oldest brick lighthouse on the Great Lakes, this tower stands 107 feet tall. Like most lucky lights this one has the advantage of being part of a state park and thereby protected. From US-31 exit at Shelby Road and head west away from the town of Shelby. Follow that to 16th Avenue and head north, zigzagging over to 18th Avenue. Follow that to Silver Lake Road and take it toward the lake and the light. You will have to pay a fee to access the state park, but remember that part of your fee goes toward the light's protection. The original Third Order lens remains in place.*

25 White River

☐ Visited on

_____

Established: 1875
Status: Inactive; museum
Location: (MI) Mouth of White Lake, just west of Whitehall
Type: Octagonal/integral brick tower and dwelling
Access: Car
About the Light: *This light was purchased and preserved and is now a museum open to the public. Access is gained by taking US-31 to the town of Whitehall and exiting at White Lake Drive. Follow that to South Shore and that in turn to Murray Road and the light. Upon decommissioning the light, the Coast Guard placed a selling price of $6,250 on the entire site, but the local township did not have that reserve cash amount in its budget. Local citizens then pooled their spare cash and provided the township the funds that allowed the light to be saved.*

26 Muskegon South Pierhead

☐ Visited on

_____

Established: (1852) 1903
Status: Active
Location: (MI) End of south pier
Type: Conical, cast iron
Access: Car
About the Light: One of Lake Michigan's "red" lights, this tower stands alone on the end of the concrete pier. The walls are cast iron and loom 53 feet high. This site is an active aid to navigation and is not open to the public. To get near the light, follow US-31 to Muskegon and find Sherman Boulevard, follow that to Beach Street and the light.

27 Grand Haven

☐ Visited on
_____

Established: (1839) Outer 1875, Inner 1905
Status: Active
Location: (MI) South shore of the Grand River, on the pier.
Type: Square integral and Conical
Access: Car
About the Light: *This site is a combination of two lights. The outer light is a wood building sheathed in steel and the inner light is a conical cast iron tower. Both are painted red and are connected by a catwalk. Most buildings such as the one on the* outer light were not constructed to house keeper's and their families, although they could do so. These big buildings actually were built to house giant marine boilers that powered their steam fog signals. Exit US-31 at Franklin Street and locate South Harbor Drive to begin your trek toward the lighthouse. Following that will lead to the light.

28 Holland

☐ Visited on
_____

Established:(1872, 1880) 1907, 1936
Status: Active
Location: (MI) End of south inner pier
Type: Square/integral, cast iron
Access: Car/foot but very restricted
About the Light: *Called "Big Red," this structure was not always as it appears today. It evolved from a simple wood tower to a larger steel tower to the present building. This building was another of those needed to house giant boilers to power that sta-* tion's steam fog signal. The site is best viewed from across the channel at Holland State park. Access to the light itself is very restricted as private property must be crossed.

29 South Haven

☐ Visited on
_____

Established: (1872) 1903
Status: Active
Location: (MI) End of south pier
Type: Conical, cast iron
Access: Car
About the Light: *South Haven itself has become a recreation Mecca. The streets are lined with gift shops and some of the best eating establishments in Michigan. Recreational boaters have taken over a waterfront that once belonged to the Great Lakes* maritime industry. Summer art fairs decorate the pier and the maritime museum is well worth the trip. As a part of all this, the cast iron light adds significantly to the atmosphere. Like many of the Lake Michigan "pier" lights, this one has a catwalk access and is painted red. From US-31 follow Water Street to the light.

30 St. Joseph North Pier ☐ Visited on

Established: (1832, 1859, 1898)
1907
Status: Active
Location: (MI) Mouth of the St. Joseph River on
north pier
Type: Cylindrical/Octagonal integral, cast iron
Access: Car/foot from Tiscornia Park
About the Light: *This site actually consists of a
pair of lights on the same pier. Both of the current lights were constructed in 1907, and
mark the entrance to the St. Joseph River. Both lights have their original Fresnel lenses
in service. The lights can be accessed by way of the pier in calm weather.*

31 St. Joseph Lighthouse Depot ☐ Visited on

Established: 1893
Status: Restaurant and Brewery
Location: (MI) Mouth of St. Joseph River on north shore
Type: Brick
Access: Car
About the Light: *The building was used as a supply, storage and
repair facility by the Lighthouse service until 1917. In 1918, it
was transferred to the Navy Department and used by the Naval
Reserve. Around 1952, it began to be used by the Army Reserve.
From 1956-1993, it housed the Michigan Army National Guard. On February 26, 1996,
it was purchased by the developers of the Lighthouse Depot Brew Pub and Restaurant
which opened for business in September, 1997.*

32 Old Michigan City ☐ Visited on

Established: (1837) 1858
Status: Inactive; museum
Location: (IN) Michigan City, Indiana,
Washington Park
Type: Integral/replica tower, brick structure
Access: Car
About the Light: *Up until 1904, this was the light
for the port of Michigan City. That season, how-
ever, the Pierhead Light was constructed and this site was abandoned. In 1973, the
lantern room and tower were replicated and placed back upon the former lighthouse.
That act succeeded in the restoration of the site, which is currently a museum. From US-
35, take US-12 and follow Pine Street to Washington Park and the light. The same directions will get you to the Pierhead Light.*

33 Michigan City East Pier

☐ Visited on

_____

Established: 1904
Status: Active
Location: (IN) Outer pierhead
Type: Octagonal/integral
Access: Car
About the Light: *In 1904, this light was construct-
ed to replace the old light which rested on the
mainland. The 49-foot-tall tower is integral to a giant fog signal building that housed
the boilers for the steam signal. In 1960 the station was automated and keepers no
longer made the trek along the elevated catwalk to access the light. This is an active
Coast Guard facility and is not open to the public.*

34 Gary Breakwater

☐ Visited on

_____

Established: 1911
Status: Active
Location: (IN) End of west pier
Type: Conical
Access: Boat
About the Light: *Since this light isn't much to look at, this is
probably only an attraction to the more enthusiastic light buffs.
Just over 40 feet tall, the steel structure is painted red and is
normally in a state of corrosion. Best access is gained by boat
as access by land is blocked by a very large industrial complex.*

35 Buffington Breakwater

☐ Visited on

_____

Established: 1926
Status: Active; private aid to navigation
Location: (IN) End of the breakwall at Buffington harbor
Type: Conical, steel
Access: Boat
About the Light: *Like the nearby Gary Breakwater light, this
light is in a state of fret. Painted red, the steel tower is elevated
to 50 feet above the lake and stands at the end of the rip-rap
stone breakwall. Best access is gained by boat as access by land
is blocked by a very large industrial complex.*

36 Indiana Harbor East Breakwater

☐ Visited on

_____

Established: 1935
Status: Active
Location: (IN) Indiana Harbor
Type: "Arts Decoratifs," or art deco.
Access: Boat
About the Light: *Constructed atop an arched concrete base, this art deco styled pylon light is similar to the Gravelly Shoal light over on Lake Huron. A plastic 375mm optic is elevated to 75 feet above the lake by the tower. A care-worn catwalk leads to the light, and this site is not open to the public. This light is identical to the Port Washington, Wisconsin, breakwater light. Direct access is blocked by a large industrial complex.*

37 Chicago Harbor

☐ Visited on

_____

Established: (1832, 1852, 1858) 1893
Status: Active
Location: (IL) South end of the north breakwater, Chicago Harbor
Type: Conical/integral, cast iron
Access: Boat
About the Light: *This steel tower was brick-lined for strength and insulation. The tower stands 48 feet tall and was placed at its present location in 1893. This is an active Coast Guard navigational aid and no public access is allowed. In modern times, the majority of commercial lake traffic is attracted into South Chicago and most of the vessels that pass this light are of a recreational nature.*

38 Chicago Harbor Southeast Guidewall

☐ Visited on

_____

Established: 1938
Status: Active
Location: (IL) Chicago lock, mouth of Chicago River
Type: Pyramidal steel tower/skeletal base
Access: Boat/restricted
About the Light: *Used to mark part of the breakwall outside of Navy Pier, this light is a simple steel box on a skeletal base. A standard lantern room lends the only appeal in viewing the site. It is part of an active Army Corps of Engineers site which operates the lock at the mouth of the Chicago River to control the water level in the river and reduces the river's flow, preventing discharge of sewage into Lake Michigan. A boat is needed to get a close look.*

39 Grosse Point

☐ Visited on

_____

Established: 1873
Status: Active; museum
Location: (IL) Evanston, Illinois
Type: Conical
Access: Foot
About the Light: *Another of those classic O.M. Poe designed lights, this wonderful tower stretches 113 feet toward the sky. In 1914 the original bricks,* which were beginning to deteriorate, were covered with a jacket of cement. This light was automated in 1935 and today is operated privately by the city of Evanston's Lighthouse Park District. The original Second Order lens remains in place. To get there, take Interstate 94 to the Old Orchard exit. Follow Old Orchard to the end then go left two blocks onto Central Street. Follow that to the light.

40 Waukegan Harbor (Little Fort)

☐ Visited on

_____

Established: (1849, 1860) 1889
Status: Active
Location: (IL) End of south pier
Type: Conical, cast iron
Access: Car
About the Light: *The lantern room is now missing, as is the attached fog signal building which was* added in 1905. Both were removed after a severe fire on June 1, 1967.

41 Kenosha Lighthouse (Southport)

☐ Visited on

_____

Established: (1848, 1858) 1866
Status: Inactive; private residence
Location: (WI) North bank of river mouth
Type: Conical, brick
Access: Car
About the Light: *In 1903, the construction of the pierhead lights made this light redundant. Deactivated in 1906, the site continued to serve as a storm warning tower from 1913 until 1953. The station was placed on the National Register as an historic site in 1975. The original cream colored brick tower and keeper's quarters continue to stand. A replica of the lantern room was added in 1994. Currently the lighthouse is managed by the Kenosha Water and Utility company.*

42 Kenosha North Pier

☐ Visited on

_____

Established: (1864) 1906
Status: Active
Location: (WI) End of North Pier
Type: Conical, cast iron
Access: Car
About the Light: *This light stands 50 feet above the lake. It's lantern room now contains a standard airport beacon and is automated. The lighthouse is located on the end of a pier, and can be accessed by foot. The lighthouse is painted red much the same as many other lights on Lake Michigan.*

43 Racine North Breakwater

☐ Visited on

_____

Established: (1839, 1866) 1912
Status: Inactive
Location: (WI) End of north pier
Type: Pyramidal steel/skeletal base
Access: Boat
About the Light: *Although this red monster may look like little more than a candidate for the scrap heap, to the locals it is a beloved landmark. The Coast Guard had scheduled the site for demolition in the late 1980s, but public outcry saved the site. Directly accessible only by boat, a very close view can be had from the park area at the end of the south pier.*

44 Wind Point

☐ Visited on

_____

Established: 1880
Status: Active
Location: (WI) 3.5 miles north of Racine Harbor
Type: Conical, brick and attached dwelling
Access: Car
About the Light: *Another of the classic "Poe" style lights, this brick tower stands 108 feet tall and is very similar in construction to the Grosse Point tower. Although only the grounds are open to the public, the keeper's quarters are sometimes used for town meetings. To get to the light, take Lighthouse Drive, and you will find the site across from Windridge Drive. It is owned by the village of Wind Point as of 1997, which had been leasing it since automation in 1964.*

45 Milwaukee Pierhead

☐ Visited on
_____

Established: (1872) 1906
Status: Active
Location: (WI) End of north pier
Type: Conical, cast iron
Access: Car
About the Light: _Another of Lake Michigan's red lights, it stands just 42 feet tall. Although the site was established in 1872, the current structure was erected in 1906. Access to this light can be had via the park area at the north bank of the river's mouth._

46 Milwaukee Breakwater

☐ Visited on
_____

Established: 1926
Status: Active
Location: (WI) End of the outer breakwater.
Type: Square/integral, steel and concrete
Access: Boat
About the Light: _Hunched on a concrete base, the light is made of concrete and steel. The four-story tower is integrated into a two-story building and is still an active navigation aid. This site is not open to the public and any venture out onto the detached breakwall is not recommended._

47 North Point

☐ Visited on
_____

Established: (1855, 1888) 1912
Status: Active
Location: (WI) Three miles north of Milwaukee
Type: Octagonal, cast iron and steel
Access: Car
About the Light: _Like the Washington Monument, a keen eye will see that this tower is in two pieces. The original 30-foot-tall tower was encroached upon by local trees in the early 1900s. With that in mind, in 1912 the tower was raised an additional 35 feet to its present appearance. The original brick structure was modified to this cast iron monster in 1888, and the 1912 extension added on to the tower. Only the surrounding grounds are open to the public. From Milwaukee, head for Lake Park and you will find the light._

48 Port Washington Breakwater

☐ Visited on

Established: (1889) 1935
Status: Active
Location: (WI) End of north pier
Type: "Arts Decoratifs," or art deco, steel and concrete
Access: Car/boat
About the Light: *This light is identical to the Indiana Harbor East Breakwater light. Since access across the breakwater is not recommended because the site is an active navigation aid and the trip out can be treacherous, it is best viewed by boat.*

49 Old Port Washington Light

☐ Visited on

Established: (1849) 1860
Status: Inactive; museum
Location: (WI) Bluff north of harbor, end of Johnson Street
Type: Brick building
Access: Car
About the Light: *Located inland from the lakefront, this building once supported the tower of the original Port Washington light. Closed after the 1935 light was built, the Coast Guard removed the lantern room from the old lighthouse to eliminate confusion. Today it is undergoing restoration and houses the offices of the Port Washington Historical Society.*

50 Manitowoc

☐ Visited on

Established: (1840, 1895) 1918
Status: Active
Location: (WI) End of north breakwater
Type: Square/integral steel and concrete
Access: Car
About the Light: *This light looks like a wedding cake. Constructed of concrete, the light tower itself is erected atop a single-story structure which rises out of a lower level fog signal building that in turn is mounted on a massive crib. This whole ordeal stands 52 feet above the lake. The light was automated in 1971 but is currently an active Coast Guard facility. A good view can also be had from the south breakwater.*

51 Two Rivers North Pierhead

Established: 1883
Status: Inactive; museum display
Location: (WI) Jackson Street Fishing Village Museum
Type: Pyramidal wooden tower
Access: Car
About the Light: *Only the top 15 feet of the pictured site is from the actual lighthouse. The rest is simply a display stand. The light was deactivated in 1969 and given to the town to use as a display 20 years later. Originally built on the end of the north pier, it was removed after a new steel tower was built and donated to the city. Get there by taking Highway 147 and crossing the 22nd Street bridge. The display is located at the marina near the river.*

52 Two Rivers Point (Rawley Point)

Established: (1853) 1894
Status: Active
Location: (WI) North of Two Rivers at Beach State Park
Type: Skeletal
Access: Car
About the Light: *Although this site was established as early as 1853, the present light was transferred to this station in 1894 from Chicago. This facility is currently used as quarters for Coast Guard personnel and their dependents and is not open to the public. The light is adjacent to the Point Beach State Forest and Park and can be viewed by entering the park and walking the beach. The entrance to the park has on display a large piece of a wooden shipwreck which washed up on the beach in the summer of 1967.*

53 Kewaunee Pierhead

Established: (1891) 1909, 1931
Status: Active
Location: (WI) End of south pier
Type: Square/integral cast iron
Access: Car
About the Light: *Standing 43 feet tall, the tower of this facility contains its original Fifth Order Fresnel lens. The fog signal building that is attached to the light tower and is typical of those found along the Lake Michigan coast. Currently, the site is an active Coast Guard property and is not open to the public. It is nearly identical to "Big Red" in Holland, Michigan, except this light is painted white.*

54 Algoma Pierhead

☐ Visited on

Established: 1932 (1893, 1908)
Status: Active
Location: (WI) End of the north pier
Type: Conical, cast iron and steel
Access: Boat
About the Light: *In 1932, the entire 26-foot-tall structure was raised to a height of 42 feet by placing the older 1908 tower on a new steel base. It was automated in 1973. The best access is to go out onto the south breakwall and look across the channel.*

55 Sturgeon Bay Ship Canal

☐ Visited on

Established: (1899) 1903
Status: Active
Location: (WI) Entrance to the Sturgeon Bay Ship Canal, Lake Michigan side
Type: Skeletal
Access: Car
About the Light: *Most sources agree that this original tower was heavily reconstructed in 1903. The light is an active Coast Guard aid to navigation and so is not open to the public. From Hwy 42-57, turn east just north of Bay View Bridge onto Utah Street, right onto Cove Road, then left on Canal Road to the station.*

56 Sturgeon Bay Ship Canal North Pierhead

☐ Visited on

Established: (1882) 1903
Status: Active
Location: (WI) Entrance pier, Sturgeon Bay Ship Canal
Type: Round/integral, cast iron and concrete
Access: Boat
About the Light: *Like its companion light ashore, this original tower was also heavily reconstructed in 1903. Elevated 43 feet high, the structure is another of Lake Michigan's big red lighthouses. The massive fog signal building makes this light easy to spot from almost anyplace nearby. This light is an active Coast Guard aid to navigation and so is not open to the public. A good view can be had from the south pierhead.*

57 Old Bailey's Harbor

☐ Visited on

_____

Established: 1851
Status: Inactive; private residence
Location: (WI) Small island at SE edge of harbor
Type: Conical, rough stone
Access: Boat
About the Light: *From the time it was built, Lake captains considered it very poorly placed, and it was finally replaced by a set of range lights in 1869. Now a private cottage, its significance lies in the fact that it retains one of only three "bird-cage" style* lantern rooms left on the Great Lakes. To reach the site, take Highway 57 north through Bailey's Harbor and exit at Ridges Road, which runs around the harbor. At the end of the road you will see the abandoned lighthouse on an island just off the mainland.

58 Bailey's Harbor Front Range

☐ Visited on

_____

Established: 1869
Status: Inactive
Location: (WI) On Ridges Road just east of Hwy 57
Type: Square/integral
Access: Car
About the Light: *It is said that these two range lights are apparently identical to the Presque Isle Range lights located over on Lake Huron. The front range was located in an over-sized booth-like structure. The range was deactivated in 1969 and currently* acts as part of the Ridges Wildlife Sanctuary and thus is not open to the public.

58 Bailey's Harbor Rear Range

☐ Visited on

_____

Established: 1869
Status: Inactive; private residence
Location: (WI) On Ridges Road just east of Hwy 57
Type: Roof-mounted cupola on wooden dwelling
Access: Car
About the Light: *It is said that these two range lights are apparently identical to the Presque Isle Range lights located over on Lake Huron. The rear range is mounted atop a schoolhouse-looking one-story wood-framed building. The range was deactivated in 1969 and currently acts as part of the Ridges Wildlife Sanctuary and thus is not open to the public.*

134

59 Cana Island

Established: 1870
Status: Active
Location: (WI) 5 miles north of Bailey's Harbor
Type: Conical, brick sheathed in cast iron plates
Access: Car
About the Light: *Steel sheaths the bricks that are the main body of this tower. Standing 81 feet high, the white tower contains a Third Order Optic. The grounds are maintained by Door County Maritime Museum. Access the site by taking County Track "Q"* to 8800 Cana Island Road and the light. Bring waterproof boots; the causeway that leads out to the island is usually under water and can be quite uneven.

60 Plum Island Front Range

Established: (1897) 1964
Status: Active
Location: (WI) Southeast side of Plum Island
Type: Skeletal
Access: Boat
About the Light: *These lights are on the lake side of Death's Door passage. Oddly, the year prior to their placement, a United States Lifesaving Service station was placed on this island. Apparently, the need for the presence of the storm warriors was* greater than the need for a light. In 1964, the original wooden front range light tower was replaced with a steel skeleton tower.

60 Plum Island Rear Range

Established: 1897
Status: Active
Location: (WI) Southeast end Plum Island, 1600 feet behind front light
Type: Skeletal
Access: Boat
About the Light: *Companion to the front range light, this tower now sports a brightly colored "day-marker" board. The complete range is located on a remote island in Lake Michigan, and* in largely inaccessible. These range lights, first lit on May 1, 1897, mark the way through Porte Des Morts (Death's Door Passage) for vessels entering from Lake Michigan.

61 Pilot Island (Port des Morts) ☐ Visited on _____

Established: 1858
Status: Active
Location: (WI) Pilot Island
Type: Square/integral
Access: Boat
About the Light: *The translation of the term "Port Des Morts" Passage is "Door of Death." And that is exactly how the old mariners thought of this place at the entrance to Green Bay. Unfortunately, until 1858, this short-cut often turned into a little more than a direct route to a shipwreck. The area is draped in fog in the good part of the season and lashed by gales and blizzards in the bad part of the season. Even with the light operating on this tiny island, many a lakeboat and crew met death in this place.*

62 Pottawatomie ☐ Visited on _____

Established: (1837) 1858
Status: Inactive; museum
Location: (WI) Northwest tip of Rock Island on a very high bluff
Type: Square/integral
Access: Boat
About the Light: *The best way in or out of Green Bay prior to the 1881 canal was right here at the north end of the passage. This station and its island foundation are in a highly-exposed position just northeast of Washington Island. The site is part of Rock Island State Park and is open to the public.*

63 St. Martin Island ☐ Visited on _____

Established: 1905
Status: Active
Location: (MI) Northeast side of the island.
Type: Hexagonal exoskeletal
Access: Boat
About the Light: *It is said that this is the only example of this type of light on the Great Lakes. The surrounding buildings are abandoned and the original lamp has been replaced by a 190mm optic. The light tower itself stands 75 feet tall and reportedly still contains its original clock-work turning mechanism. Access to the light is gained only by taking a boat to the island.*

64 Poverty Island

☐ Visited on

_____

Established: 1875
Status: Inactive; ruins
Location: (MI) South end of the island
Type: Conical brick tower and attached dwelling
Access: Boat
About the Light: *Having been replaced by a simple light on a pole, this site is a prime example of what happens to a neglected lighthouse. The buildings are in a state of dilapidation with some vandalism having taken place within. If concern were high enough, the remote brick lighthouse could yet be saved.*

65 Eagle Bluff

☐ Visited on

_____

Established: 1868
Status: Active; museum
Location: (WI) East channel into Green Bay
Type: Square/integral
Access: Car
About the Light: *Getting to this site requires that you take Route 42 to Shore Road. The light is in the Peninsula State Park and is open to the public. This tower stands 43 feet tall and currently it uses a solar powered light in a 300mm plastic lens to alert the passing traffic. This is a far cry from its original Third One Half Order Optic and oil-fired lamp that the original keeper, Henry Stanley, had to heat and haul fuel to.*

66 Chambers Island

☐ Visited on

_____

Established: 1868
Status: Inactive; museum
Location: (WI) In the middle of Green Bay, NW end of island
Type: Octagonal/integral brick tower and dwelling
Access: Boat
About the Light: *Leased to a private group by the Coast Guard, this site is not open to the public. The original light was placed atop the 67-foot-tall octagonal brick tower in 1868, but was replaced by a taller steel skeletal tower and light in 1961. Missing is the original lantern room, but the rest of the original structure remains. The lens now rests in a folk museum in... NEBRASKA!*

67 Sherwood Point

☐ Visited on

Established: 1883
Status: Active; private residence
Location: (WI) On the "elbow" of Sherwood Point, mouth of Sturgeon Bay.
Type: Square/integral brick tower and dwelling
Access: Car
About the Light: *"Sherwood Point Station" is an active Coast Guard facility. Its location at the* entrance to Sturgeon Bay is very strategic to modern Great Lakes shipping. The biggest of the lakeboats often use this area to visit the famed Bay Shipbuilding Yard. This station still has its original Fourth Order Fresnel lens which according to the book, The Northern Lights, *by Hyde, is said to be marked "Barbier & Fenestre, Constr. Paris, 1880." Used as a summer residence by Coast Guard personnel.*

68 Peshtigo Reef

☐ Visited on

Established: 1934
Status: Active
Location: (WI) Off Peshtigo Point in Green Bay
Type: Conical steel tower
Access: Boat
About the Light: *Unlike other lights constructed in the era of the 1930s, this structure really looks like a lighthouse. Atop the steel, conical tower is an actual lantern room that houses the beacon. The entire structure is mounted on a concrete crib and* has a total elevation of 72 feet above the water. This shoal light is not open to public access.

69 Green Bay Harbor Entrance

☐ Visited on

Established: 1935
Status: Active
Location: (WI) 9 miles north of Green Bay
Type: "Arts Decoratifs," or art deco conical steel tower
Access: Boat
About the Light: *Constructed atop a concrete pier, the tower supports a light with a 72-foot focal plane. The entire site is well off shore and is accessible only by boat. Much older aids have marked the entrance to the city of Green Bay, including three* different Longtail Point lights and the Grassy Island Range Lights below.

70 Grassy Island Front Range

Established: 1872
Status: Inactive
Location: (WI) Green Bay Yacht Club
Type: Pyramidal wooden tower
Access: Car
About the Light: *These range lights remained in service until 1966, at which time they were removed from the outer harbor entrance to make way for a dredging project. Both lights were given to the Green Bay Yacht club, which is located near the mouth of the Fox River.*

70 Grassy Island Rear Range

Established: 1872
Status: Inactive
Location: (WI) Green Bay Yacht Club
Type: Pyramidal wooden tower
Access: Car
About the Light: *These range lights remained in service until 1966, at which time they were removed from the outer harbor entrance to make way for a dredging project. Both lights were given to the Green Bay Yacht club, which is located near the mouth of the Fox River.*

71 Longtail Point (Ruins)

Established: 1849
Status: Inactive; ruins
Location: (WI) 3 miles north of Green Bay
Type: Conical rough stone
Access: Boat
About the Light: *The first of three lights to occupy Longtail Point and mark the way into Green Bay, this lighthouse was discontinued in 1859 because the lighthouse service thought it would soon topple due to water erosion. Ironically, in remains as the only one of the three to survive!*

72 Menominee North Pier

☐ Visited on

_____

Established: (1877) 1927
Status: Active
Location: (MI) End of north pier
Type: Octagonal, cast iron
Access: Car
About the Light: *Constructed of cast iron, this bright red tower will continue to stand up to the lake. The lighthouse itself is 34 feet tall and has a 46-foot focal plane. The best access is from the waterfront of the harbor. At one time, this light was attached to a fog signal building.*

73 Sand Point

☐ Visited on

_____

Established: 1868
Status: Inactive; museum
Location: (MI) Escanaba waterfront
Type: Square/integral brick and attached dwelling
Access: Car
About the Light: *This is the original building that contained the 1868 light. It was somehow built backwards, with the tower facing the town instead of the water! Damaged by a fire in 1886, it nevertheless continued in service until 1939. This site is a fully-restored lighthouse museum and its lantern room is that of the abandoned Poverty Island lighthouse. Currently the site is leased from the Coast Guard to the Delta County Historical Society. You can get there by following US-2 and 41 to Ludington Street.*

74 Minneapolis Shoal

☐ Visited on

_____

Established: 1934
Status: Active
Location: (MI) In Green Bay, 11 miles south of Escanaba
Type: "Arts Decoratifs," or art deco.
Access: Boat
About the Light: *Located over a critical obstruction that is directly on the course out of the key iron ore port of Escanaba, this light replaces a lightship stationed at this site prior to its construction in 1934. Identical to Grays Reef Light (1936), it has a lantern room and Fourth Order Fresnel lens rather than just a plastic lens erected atop the tower. The light's location is fairly remote and a boat would be needed to get to it, but a visit by air is likely the best way to access the site.*

75 Peninsula Point

☐ Visited on

Established: 1866
Status: Inactive
Location: (MI) 18 miles south of US-2 on Co. Rd. 513
Type: Square
Access: Car
About the Light: *Standing like a monolith, this buff-brick tower is located in the picnic portion of the Hiawatha National Forest. The site and the tower are open to the public. In 1936, when the Minneapolis Shoal Light was activated, this light was declared redundant and was then closed. The dwelling was totally destroyed by fire in 1959. Access to this light is gained by visiting the National Forest.*

76 Manistique East Breakwater

☐ Visited on

Established: 1915
Status: Active
Location: (MI) end of east breakwater
Type: Pyramidal, cast iron
Access: Car
About the Light: *Another of the red lighthouses of Lake Michigan, the light marks the port of Manistique and stands 35 feet tall. Made of steel plate, the light was automated in 1969 and currently uses a 300mm plastic lens as its optic.*

77 Seul Choix Point

☐ Visited on

Established: 1895
Status: Active; museum
Location: (MI) Sixteen miles east of Manistique.
Type: Conical brick tower and attached dwelling
Access: Car
About the Light: *Similar to the "Poe" style lights of the lakes region, this light resembles Presque Isle, South Manitou, and Au Sable Point. The tower stands 78 feet tall and is made of brick. To access the light you must follow US 2 and exit at Port Inland Road; from there seek County Road 431 to the light. Automated in 1972, this light is also the site of a museum and gift shop and is run by the Gulliver Historical Society by means of the Michigan Department of Natural Resources.*

78 Lansing Shoal

Visited on _____

Established: (1900) 1928
Status: Active
Location: (MI) Northern Lake Michigan
Type: Square/integral steel and concrete
Access: Boat
About the Light: *This site was marked by a gas buoy for several years prior to Lightship #55 going into service in July, 1900. In 1928, the current light* was constructed atop a massive concrete crib. Its Fresnel lens was removed in 1985 and is now on display at Michigan Historical Museum in Lansing. Illumination of the 190mm plastic lens is now provided by means of solar power and the site is fully automated. This site is well out in the lake and is best viewed by use of an aircraft or a substantial boat.

79 St. Helena

Visited on _____

Established: 1873
Status: Active
Location: (MI) 6 miles west of the Mackinac Bridge
Type: Conical brick and attached dwelling
Access: Boat
About the Light: *Leased to the Great Lakes Lighthouse Keepers Association, this site is opened to the public by appointment. Calling 313-436-9150 allows the light buff to arrange a visit to the station. This light acts not only as an active aid to navigation, but as a place for education in maritime heritage.* Automated in 1922, the brick tower stands 71 feet tall and currently contains a 250mm plastic optic.

THAT OL' RASCAL,
JOHN HERMAN

There are some tales that can only be told in terms of legends that have been handed down over the years. Likewise, some of the stories of lighthouses are so strange and bizarre that no one ever dared to put them into an official record. For that reason all that is left to us is hearsay and lore. This is such a tale. Considering that there is no real documentation of the events, all that was available to construct this story is pure speculation and supposition. In the entire length of the book that you are now reading, this is the only area that does not consist of documented facts, because no one was ever crazy enough to put these events into documentation. Still the tale is so much fun to tell, that leaving it out of any book of Great Lakes lighthouses would be a waste. This is the story of the ghost of the Waugoshance lighthouse.

Waugoshance shoal is just one of a peppering of islands, shoals and reefs at the northern end of Lake Michigan. The shoal itself is located directly in the path of vessels that are passing through the Straits of Mackinac, and for many years found its way into the hull timbers of assorted vessels that happened too near its rocks. In 1831 it was decided by the Lighthouse Board to establish a light at this location and the following year a lightship was stationed on the shoal. The Waugoshance lightship held the distinction of being the first lightship ever established on the Great Lakes. This lightship saw twenty seasons of service before being replaced by a lighthouse in 1852. In another first, the Waugoshance lighthouse was the first on the Great Lakes to be constructed in open water by using a submarine crib to establish a foundation. The new lighthouse had walls that were made of stone and measured five and one half feet thick. In 1883 it was discovered that these walls were suffering from the weather and an iron sheathing was bolted around the tower. This sheath was day-marked with vertical red stripes and was expected to add greatly to the life span of the site. Then came Lighthouse Keeper John Herman.

143

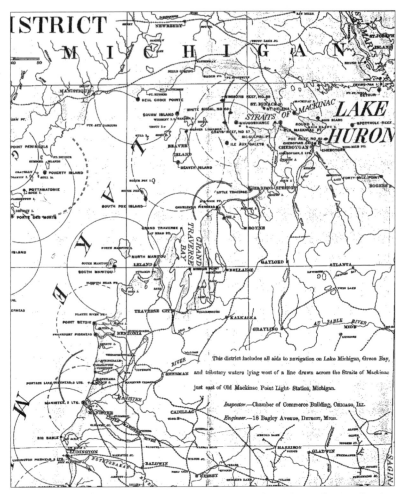

1896 Lighthouse Board Map of Lake Michigan and Mackinac Straits showing Waugoshance Light.

Not a lot is on record about keeper Herman, but hearsay indicates that he was a jovial individual who enjoyed his job. It is also said that Herman also enjoyed his drink. In an era when temperance was fast becoming the most fashionable way of life, and in a job where, if you were caught, there was very little tolerance for drinking on the job, John Herman was said to have kept more than his light well fueled. Once under the influence of distilled products, Keeper Herman was prone to pulling practical jokes of every sort. Considering his taste for the grape, it should be noted that Keeper Herman's light was always faithfully in working order. Realistically, so long as his light and fog horn were working when needed, the Lighthouse Board was willing to look the other way when it came to any of his "other" activities.

In 1894, Keeper Herman had been sipping a bit at that little brown jug, and had gotten into another dual of practical joking with his assistant lightkeeper. At one point, the assistant keeper had gone into the lantern room to attend to the light, and Keeper Herman sneaked up behind him and slammed the iron trapdoor that led into the room. Slamming the door and throwing the bolt, Keeper Herman dashed down the stairway laughing in drunken glee. By the time that the assistant keeper managed to free himself from the lantern room, John Herman was nowhere to be found. The conclusion was later drawn that Keeper Herman had simply walked off the pier in a drunken stupor and was swallowed by Lake Michigan, never again to be seen.

In the years that followed, Keepers of the Waugoshance light began to experience a number of strange happenings. In one case, coal was found shoveled into the fog signal's boilers when no one had been in the coal room. Later keepers stated that if anyone were to fall asleep while on duty, they would be rudely awakened either by a slamming door or by having their chair kicked out from under them. The hauntings continued and got so bad that it was said that keepers were refusing to do duty out on Waugoshance light. In 1910, when the White Shoals light, which was located five miles to the northwest, opened, it was decided that Waugoshance was obsolete. The light was later abandoned, and during World War II it was given the extreme insult of being used as a bombing target. Perhaps this was one way for the government to rid itself of John Herman.

Today, the light remains standing with just the skeleton of its lantern room and the bare rocks of its tower to face the elements. Perhaps John Herman still tends the site, perhaps it is all just a yarn. The Waugoshance lighthouse is in a remote area and is accessible only by boat or aircraft, and then only during a short span of the season. Whether or not the ghost of John Herman really exists is a hard question for those of us with a scientific background to answer. All that I can say for a fact is that while writing this piece, my computer's spell-checker decided to stop working. There could be a zillion explanations for this, from a stray cosmic ray to... that ol' rascal John Herman. I hope that the publisher has better luck with this tale, and their computer equipment.

THE
LIGHTS
OF LAKE
SUPERIOR

GREAT LAKES LIGHTHOUSES

1 Frying Pan Island

2 Pipe Island

3 Round Island

4 Point Iroquois

5 Whitefish Point

6 Crisp Point

7 Grand Marais Front
   Range

8 Grand Marais Rear
   Range

9 Au Sable Point

10 Grand Island Old
   North

11 Grand Island East
   Channel

12 Munising Range
   Front

13 Munising Range Rear

14 Grand Island Harbor
   Rear Range

15 Marquette Harbor
   Light

16 Presque Isle Harbor
   Breakwater

17 Granite Island

18 Stannard's Rock

19 Big Bay Point

20 Huron Island

21 Sand Point

22 Portage River

23 Keweenaw Waterway

24 Mendota (Bete Grise)

25 Gull Rock

26 Manitou

27 Copper Harbor

28 Copper Harbor Rear
   Range

29 Eagle Harbor

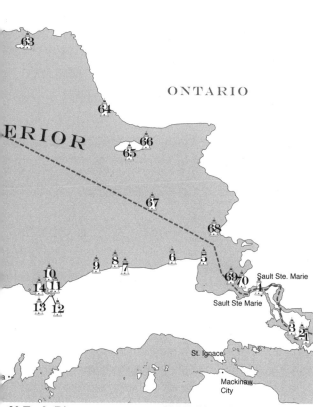

Lake Superior

Aptly named, Lake Superior is, without question, the largest and the deepest of all of the Great Lakes. Depths on the big lake can measure more than 1,200 feet, or almost as deep as the 1,250 foot Empire State building is tall. One giant 10 by 20 mile, comma-shaped hole just east of the Keweenaw Peninsula is more than 170 fathoms, or 1,020 feet deep. To make a comparison here, the largest vessel on the Great Lakes, the 1,013 foot long PAUL R. TREGURTHA could be placed on end in this spot and still have more than 7 feet of water over her. Another fun example of this spot is that the entire city of Detroit could be submerged here and there would still be about 270 feet of Lake Superior covering the Renaissance Center. The topography of Lake Superior's ice-age bottom also does some amazing things. From nearly the beginning of navigation on the big lake, mariners had spoken of the legend of the "pinnacle of doom" that lurked in mid lake. It was said that this uncharted spike of rock suddenly loomed from great depths and waited just below the surface to snag an unsuspecting boat that would stumble upon it in a storm. Not until the second decade of the 1900s was it discovered that the legendary "pinnacle of doom" actually existed. It is called Superior Shoal and is located 46 miles from the nearest land and truly does just rise up from the depths. In fact, the water depth goes from 420 feet to only 21 feet in less than 3 miles distance from the shoal. On a lake where storm seas are often above 20 feet, a boat can be sailing in more than 400 feet of water, then hit bare rock, gut herself, and sail right back into more than 700 feet of water in less than eight miles distance! Lake Superior's depths are awesome to ponder, even in modern times.

Aside from being deep, Lake Superior is also cold, and surrounded by some of the most remote and rugged coastline imaginable. The Michigan, Wisconsin and Minnesota coastline of the lake is one of the most isolated inhospitable shores in the United States, second only to that of Alaska. The entire region has a weather pattern that consists of eight months of winter and four months of poor sledding. In this area, hard weather towns such as Sault Saint Marie and Marquette are considered to be "southern cities" by the folks who reside in places such as Nipigon and Thunder Bay. Looking at a map you will find that the southern most point of Lake Superior itself is the city of Munising, Michigan which is nearly halfway between the earth's 46th and 47th parallels.

The first French explorers on Lake Superior called it "Grand Lac," as indicated by the maps of Samuel de Champlain. Later the term "le lac sup'erieur," meaning "upper lake" was applied, which appears to be where the current name of the lake was taken.

Lore abounds of Lake Superior, because it truly is a treacherous place. Average temperature of the lake's water is just over 40 degrees Fahrenheit and this has led to the saying that, "Superior never gives up her dead." It is the truth, because bodies lost in the lake are cooled to the point where the bacteria that causes a corpse to bloat and float to the surface, cannot survive or grow. Thus, most of those who have found their fate in Lake Superior simply sink to the bottom and are mummified there. Northern gales seem always to rampage most freely on Lake Superior. Being 161 miles wide from Au Train to Bottle Point, and 303 miles long from Agawa Bay to the Duluth Ship Canal, the big lake's surface is prone to waves that can exceed 40 feet tall in any substantial blow from most directions. To add to the Lake Superior mystique came the November 10th, 1975 wreck of the oreboat EDMUND FITZGERALD, and the songs, books, mugs, T-shirts, T.V. shows, plays, posters, paintings and trinkets that followed. Lake lore has it that this was the loss of the largest boat on the lakes.

Such is not exactly true; the loss of the largest boat on the lakes occurred on September 5, 1964 when the oreboat LEECLIFFE HALL collided with the Greek freighter APOLLONIA in the St. Lawrence River and later sank. Technically, the St. Lawrence is considered part of the Great Lakes, and technically, the HALL was 730 feet long, while the "FITZ" was only 729 feet long. Perspective on this detail all depends on the school of boat-nut to which you may belong. The fact is that the wreck of the FITZ, the most-publicized disaster in Great Lakes maritime history, has managed to draw thousands of new boat-buffs into the maritime history circle.

Major navigation on Lake Superior did not begin until the opening of the first lock at Sault Saint Marie in 1855. From that moment on there was no stopping the flow of iron ore from the rich "range" cities around the lake. Vessel traffic exploded and the commerce of the Superior shores boomed. A direct result of this late start in the maritime boom is that the lighthouses of Lake Superior are much younger than many of their lower lakes counterparts. These lights are no less elegant and historic, however. The most isolated lights on the lakes are found in the Lake Superior region. It is a sure bet that if the cold breath of the Lake Superior wind does not take your breath away, the scenery will.

1 Frying Pan Island

☐ Visited on

Established: 1887
Status: Inactive
Location: (MI) In front of Sault Ste. Marie Coast Guard
Station
Type: Cast iron
Access: Car
About the Light: *Moved for display to this site when the modern structure still in use on the Island was placed in service. Just downriver from DeTour Village, Frying Pan Island was once used as a coal fueling station for bulk steamers.*

2 Pipe Island

☐ Visited on

Established: 1888
Status: Active; island privately owned
Location: (MI) Southern edge of Pipe Island
Type: Octagonal brick tower with steel-skeleton
Access: Boat
About the Light: *Built by the Lake Carriers Association to aid shipping entering the St. Marys River from the open waters of Lake Huron. The tower was extended in height by the steel skeleton atop the original structure in 1937. Access to the island is restricted as it is privately owned.*

3 Round Island

☐ Visited on

Established: 1892
Status: Inactive; privately owned
Location: (MI) Lower Saint Marys River, just above Lime Island
Type: Square/integral
Access: Boat
About the Light: *There are hundreds of "lights" that the mariners use to aid in navigating the Saint Marys River. Even today, the lake mariners use known porch lights, yard lights and street lights to align their vessels in the narrow channels. Such "home-made" navigational aids are not officially charted, but exist in the memories of every vessel master, mate and wheelsman. This light is located on a small island smack in the channel. It is a wood framed site and was replaced by a nearby steel light on a post with a plastic lens.*

4 Point Iroquois

☐ Visited on

_____

Established: (1855) 1871
Status: Inactive; museum
Location: (MI) Mouth of the Saint Marys River, above the locks
Type: Conical brick tower
Access: Car
About the Light: *With the "State Lock" about to open in 1855, it was decided that the new load of vessel traffic would require a light at Point Iroquois where that expanse of Whitefish Bay suddenly funnels into the river and takes a sudden "U" turn, redirecting the channel from south back to a heading of nearly north and on to the Soo. In 1870, the tower which exists today was constructed, and the station was extinguished in 1962, being replaced by Gros Cap Reef light in the Canadian channel. Today the site is managed by the U.S. Forest Service and is open to the public and has a gift shop.*

5 Whitefish Point

☐ Visited on

_____

Established: (1849) 1861
Status: Active
Location: (MI) Tip of Whitefish Point
Type: Skeletal
Access: Car
About the Light: *A critical place for lake mariners is Whitefish Point. Not only is it the turning point for vessel traffic in and out of Superior, but also is the only shelter within 75 miles of the open lake. Many a lakeboat has struggled to reach the point. Some have never made the distance needed to find the shelter. This light and surrounding buildings have been restored to one of the best maritime and lighthouse museums on the Great Lakes. There is a gift shop as well. On display is the actual bell of the EDMUND FITZGERALD, removed from the wreck and restored in 1995.*

6 Crisp Point

☐ Visited on

_____

Established: 1904
Status: Inactive
Location: (MI) 14 miles west of Whitefish Point
Type: Conical brick tower
Access: Car
About the Light: *Automated in 1947, this site was once the location of a United States Lifesaving Service station established in 1876, long before the construction of the light. Today, only the 58-foot-tall lighthouse remains. The U.S.L.S. station was closed in 1930. In 1965, all of the buildings except the lighthouse were razed by the Coast Guard, and the light finally deactivated in 1989. This is a lonely stretch of beach, and it is only that isolation that has spared the lighthouse from being destroyed by vandals. Getting there requires following County Road 412... forever! (18 miles off main road).*

7 Grand Marais Front Range

☐ Visited on

_____

Established: 1895
Status: Active
Location: (MI) North end of pier
Type: Steel pyramidal/skeletal
Access: Car
About the Light: *Of the two range towers, this one was constructed three years prior to the installation of the rear range light. Grand Marais is the only harbor of refuge between Whitefish Bay and Munising.*

8 Grand Marais Rear Range

☐ Visited on

_____

Established: 1898
Status: Active
Location: (MI) South (inner) end of pier
Type: Steel pyramidal/skeletal
Access: Car
About the Light: *This light was erected in 1898. To access the range, drive toward the town of Grand marais on Highway 58 and take County Road 702 to the waterfront museum and the range lights.*

9 Au Sable Point

☐ Visited on

_____

Established: 1874
Status: Active
Location: (MI) 31 miles east of Munising
Type: Conical brick tower and attached dwelling
Access: Car/then hike by foot
About the Light: *Protected among the Pictured Rocks National Lakeshore, this is another of the "Poe" style towers. Standing 87 feet tall, this beautiful light is fending off time much better than its neighbor at Crisp Point. The National Park Service is currently restoring this site and it is open to the public. Driving H-58 to the Pictured Rocks National Lakeshore will lead you toward the site. Park rangers will direct you to the light from there. Another way to access the site is to drive west 12 miles on H-58 from Grand Marais to the Hurricane River Campground and hike 1.5 miles from there.*

10 Grand Island Old North

☐ Visited on
_____

Established: (1855) 1867
Status: Inactive; private residence
Location: (MI) North side of Grand Island
Type: Square/integral brick
Access: Ferry
About the Light: *This light and the property around it are privately owned and access is strictly limited. Grand Island itself protects the harbor of Munising from the rantings of Lake Superior, and so a light marking this area was badly needed.*

Today, the vessels of lake commerce, other than those of fishermen, rarely use this as shelter and the light is not needed. The light was deactivated and a modern structure erected in 1961.

11 Grand Island East Channel

☐ Visited on
_____

Established: 1868
Status: Inactive/near-ruins
Location: (MI) Southeast shore of Grand Island
Type: Square/integral wooden tower
Access: Boat
About the Light: *This light is one of the most endangered sites on the lakes. The wood-framed lighthouse was abandoned in 1913 and has been weathering away since that time. Board by board, the Lake Superior climate is now taking the light apart.*

In spite of some local efforts to save this structure, soon this light will collapse upon itself and only photos of the station will remain. The light and the property around it are privately owned.

12 Munising Range Front

☐ Visited on
_____

Established: 1908
Status: Active
Location: (MI) West end of Munising Bay.
Type: Conical cast iron
Access: Car
About the Light: *This site consists of a pair of lighthouses. The front range light is a tower that is blinded to provide the range beam. This tower is made of riveted iron plate and stands 50 feet tall. The second, or rear range light, is located farther inland and stands upon a small hill. This tower is 30 feet tall. By lining up on the two lamps, mariners can navigate within the channel.*

13 Munising Range Rear

☐ Visited on
_____

Established: 1908
Status: Active
Location: (MI) Uphill from Front Range Light
Type: Conical cast iron
Access: Car
About the Light: *This is the most inland of the two lights in the range. It is 58 feet tall and constructed of iron plate. Interestingly, locomotive headlights are used as illumination at this site.*

14 Grand Island Harbor Rear Range

☐ Visited on
_____

Established: (1868) 1914
Status: Inactive
Location: (MI) Just south of Hwy M-28 near Christmas
Type: Conical cast iron
Access: Car
About the Light: *This metal tower replaced in earlier wood frame tower and attached dwelling which were built in 1868. It was deactivated in 1969. The top 32 feet of this light once stood at another location near the Soo Locks. The light was transferred to the U.S. Forest Service in 1977. This range marked the narrow channel west of Grand Island leading into Munising. The front range light, a modern structure, is still active.*

15 Marquette Harbor Light

☐ Visited on
_____

Established: (1853) 1866
Status: Active
Location: (MI) Just north of the Marquette downtown waterfront.
Type: Square/integral brick
Access: Car/foot
About the Light: *From the downtown harbor front, this light can be seen as it sits atop a massive rock. The scene is somewhat like that of a castle on the lake. Both the light and its attached quarters are an imposing sight. This is an active Coast Guard station and access to the public is not permitted, but you can get close. Visiting the local maritime museum and gift shop will allow you to get close enough to walk within photo distance of the station.*

16 Presque Isle Harbor Breakwater

☐ Visited on

_____

Established: 1941
Status: Active
Location: (MI) End of breakwater
Type: Cylindrical steel and concrete
Access: Boat
About the Light: This light is located at the end of a long break-water at Presque Isle, Marquette's beautiful island sanctuary and the upper harbor, home to a very active ore dock. During rough weather the breakwater is *extremely* dangerous. Although a popular walking sight in fair weather, it has numerous times claimed lives and should be absolutely avoided in rough weather.

17 Granite Island

☐ Visited on

_____

Established: 1868
Status: Inactive
Location: (MI) 11 miles north of Marquette
Type: Square/integral granite blocks
Access: Boat
About the Light: This style of lighthouse is very common on Lake Superior, but the materials used to construct these "schoolhouse" lights differ con-siderably. The Grand Island East Channel light is made of wood, the Grand Island North light is made of brick and this light is made, appropriately, of cut granite. The site is still under the management of the Coast Guard because the adjacent light on a pole is an active navigational aid. As a result of the property's status, it is not open to public access.

18 Stannard's Rock*

☐ Visited on

_____

Established: 1882
Status: Active
Location: (MI) 44 miles due north of Marquette
Type: Conical granite blocks
Access: Boat [preferably a _large_ boat]
About the Light: *Stannard's Rock is another of those "pinnacles of doom" that just jut from the lake's bottom. The depth in this area goes from 546 feet to 30 inches above the surface in the space of less than two miles. This shoal was discovered very early in Lake Superior navigation on August 26, 1835, by Captain Charles C. Stannard. Official talk of placing a light there did not start until November 21, 1866, however. After the opening of the locks at the Soo. A "Day Beacon," or iron marking post, was put in place in 1868. Construction of the lighthouse itself was started in June 1877.*

*Author's note; Although most modern sources use the name "Stannard," the original documents of this light from 1877 to 1882 use the possessive form "Stannard's" so it is seen here in that form.

19 Big Bay Point

☐ Visited on

_____

Established: 1896
Status: Active; private aid to navigation
Location: (MI) 23 miles northwest of Marquette
Type: Square /integral brick
Access: Car
About the Light: *Unique is the access to this light because it has been made into a bed and breakfast resort. The true lighthouse buff can visit this light, and stay! Mailing to "Big Bay Point Lighthouse, No.3 Lighthouse Road, Big Bay MI 49808 (phone 906/345-9957) can get you information on a stay at this active lighthouse. The red brick building is attached to a tower standing 65 feet tall. The light was automated in 1945 and sold in 1961.*

20 Huron Island

☐ Visited on

_____

Established: 1868
Status: Active
Location: (MI) Three miles north of the Huron Mountains shore
Type: Square/integral granite blocks
Access: Boat
About the Light: *Nearly identical to the Granite Island light, this structure still uses its own light tower to warn passing vessels. Even though the tower is only 39 feet tall, the grounds on which the light has been constructed are so high that the focal plane, or the height that the light beam itself is elevated above the lake's surface, is 197 feet. This site is not open to the public.*

21 Sand Point

☐ Visited on

_____

Established: 1878
Status: Inactive; privately owned
Location: (MI) Southern end of L'Anse Bay
Type: Square/integral brick
Access: Car
About the Light: *Another of the "schoolhouse" style lights that are so common in this area, this structure is constructed of fine brick. The light is inactive, but the site has been converted into a private residence. This light is not open to the public.*

22 Portage River (Jacobsville)

☐ Visited on
_____

Established: (1856) 1870
Status: Inactive; private residence
Location: (MI) Portage River entrance
Type: Conical brick tower and attached dwelling
Access: Car
About the Light: _Converted into a private residence, this light is not open to the public. The tower stands 65 feet tall and has a red lantern room. Directions to this light can be gotten in the town of Jacobsville, but it is unlikely that the current owners would wish their privacy violated._

23 Keweenaw Waterway

☐ Visited on
_____

Established: (1868) 1920
Status: Active
Location: (MI) Portage River entrance
Type: Octagonal steel and concrete
Access: Car
About the Light: _Located on the east pierhead of the lower entrance to the Portage Ship Canal, this light is an active aid to navigation. Although this site was established in 1868, the existing tower was constructed in 1920. The site is operated by the Coast Guard, but is not open to the public. To get close you must drive toward Portage Lake on US 41 and turn off just after the highway veers from the lakeside. The light can be viewed from the south side of the Portage entrance._

24 Mendota (Bete Grise)

☐ Visited on
_____

Established: (1870) 1895
Status: Active; private residence
Location: (MI) Mendota Ship Channel
Type: Square /integral brick
Access: Car to edge of channel
About the Light: _From US 41 head to Lac LaBelle and from there to the town of Bete Grise and south from there to the light. This light was deactivated in 1960 and is now a private residence. The light's optic has been removed and no record exists as to its deposition. It is not open to the public. The Mendota was relit on July 5, 1998._

25 Gull Rock

☐ Visited on

Established: 1867
Status: Active
Location: (MI) Two miles due east of Keweenaw Point
Type: Square/integral brick
Access: Boat
About the Light: *Similar to the other schoolhouse lights around the lake, this site lives up to its name. The brick lighthouse stands on little more than a "rock" sticking out of Lake Superior and is a roost for seagulls. Today, the original optic has been replaced with a 250mm plastic lens, and a solar powered light. The quarters have long been abandoned and the site is not open to the public.*

26 Manitou

☐ Visited on

Established: (1850) 1861
Status: Active
Location: (MI) Seven miles off Keweenaw Point on the east side of the island
Type: Skeletal cast iron with attached wooden dwelling
Access: Boat
About the Light: *Looking very much like the Whitefish Point light, this tower stands 80 feet tall and was automated in 1935. The light's original optic has been replaced with a 190mm plastic lens. This is an active aid to navigation and the Coast Guard does not open it to the public.*

27 Copper Harbor

☐ Visited on

Established: (1849) 1866
Status: Inactive; museum
Location: (MI) East point of Copper Harbor
Type: Square/integral brick
Access: Ferry
About the Light: *Access to this light is gained by catching the boat from the west side of Copper Harbor, at the Municipal Pier. It was deactivated in 1927 and has a tower that stands 62 feet tall, but has no optic. This is a well preserved example of the schoolhouse style lighthouse. Currently the site is used as a museum, open during the summer months, which in this part of the country is any month when snow is not falling. Automated to gas in 1919, the light was moved to the current 60 foot steel tower in 1927. Remarkably, the original 1849 detached keepers house is still standing nearby!*

28 Copper Harbor Rear Range

☐ Visited on
_____

Established: 1869
Status: Inactive
Location: (MI) Access from Fort Wilkins
Type: Roof of wooden dwelling
Access: Car
About the Light: *A skeletal tower built in 1964 replaced this rear range light and a smaller tower* built in 1927 replaced the front range light. Currently, the building is used as a residence for the manager of Fort Wilkins State Park.

29 Eagle Harbor

☐ Visited on
_____

Established: (1851) 1871
Status: Active; museum
Location: (MI) West end of Eagle Harbor
Type: Octagonal brick tower and attached dwelling
Access: Car
About the Light: *Originally, this site was established in 1851, but 20 years later, the original structures were so weathered that the lighthouse board decided to construct the present lighthouse. The current tower stands 44 feet tall and painted white on one* side, but remains its original red-brick color on the land side. The site is accessed simply by driving Michigan Route 26 to Eagle Harbor. Everything there is in close proximity and you will easily find the lighthouse.

30 Eagle River

☐ Visited on
_____

Established: (1854) 1874
Status: Inactive; private residence
Location: (MI) Mouth of Eagle River
Type: Square/integral brick
Access: Car
About the Light: *The lighthouse at this site is a private residence and is not open to the public. The wood-framed house is joined with a light tower* that was deactivated in 1908.

31 Sand Hills

☐ Visited on

_____

Established: 1919
Status: Inactive
Location: (MI) North of Ahmeek at Five-Mile Point
Type: Square
Access: Car
About the Light: _Standing like a buff fortress against the ire of Lake Superior, this lighthouse has been converted into a Bed and Breakfast. (For more information or reservations, call Bill Frabotta, owner, at 906/337-1744.) The structure itself consists of two fog buildings and a tower that rises 90 feet above the lake's surface. In 1919, when the light was placed in service, this area was still well traveled by all kinds of lake vessels, but by the mid 1950s the area saw little traffic and the light was deactivated._

32 Keweenaw Upper Entrance

☐ Visited on

_____

Established: (1874) 1950
Status: Active
Location: (MI) West end of north breakwater
Type: Art-deco steel and concrete
Access: Car/foot
About the Light: _Access to this rough breakwater can be had via McClain State Park._

33 Fourteen Mile Point

☐ Visited on

_____

Established: 1894
Status: Inactive/ruins
Location: (MI) On Fourteen Mile Point
Type: Square/integral brick
Access: Boat/Foot
About the Light: _Of all of the abandoned lights on Lake Superior, this one appears as the most hopeless. Decommissioned in 1934, the site's location in the isolation of the wooded shore has not spared it from vandals. The buildings are rapidly being ravaged, and there is little hope for their preservation. In July of 1984, some mindless vandals set the lighthouse afire and now only a shell remains. This is a sad place._

34 Ontonagon

☐ Visited on
_____

Established: (1852) 1866
Status: Inactive; surrounded by private property
Location: (MI) Mouth of the Ontonagon River
Type: Square/integral, brick
Access: Car

About the Light: *Constructed of buff-colored brick, this school-house styled light is open only by appointment made with local Coast Guard Auxiliary. The site was established in 1852, but the current light was not constructed until 1866. Deactivated in 1964, the site is now under the management of the Coast Guard Auxiliary. Driving on M-38 you will find that it turns into River Street as you get into the city of Ontonagon and on that road the County Historical Museum can be found. There you can obtain directions to the lighthouse which is within sight.*

35 Ontonagon West Pierhead

☐ Visited on
_____

Established: 1897
Status: Active
Location: (MI) Mouth of Ontonagon River at end of west pier
Type: Pyramidal steel/skeletal
Access: Car/foot

About the Light: *The 20-foot-tall tower has a focal plane of 31 feet. It is the only lighted aid to navigation now marking the mouth of the river. Access, as with the main light, remains diffi-cult as it is surrounded by private property.*

36 Ashland Breakwater

☐ Visited on
_____

Established: 1915
Status: Active
Location: (WI) Northwestern tip of breakwater
Type: Hexagonal/pyramidal reinforced concrete
Access: Boat

About the Light: *The breakwall that this light is located upon arcs nearly a mile out into the lake, and so the light itself is con-structed on a base of reinforced concrete to help fight off the wild waves. Solar powered, the site is now fully automated, so no one needs to make a hazardous trip out to tend the light. The tower is 58 feet tall and has a focal plane of 60 feet. To see the light, drive along US-2 to the city of Ashland and go to Bay View Park; the tower is visible from that point.*

37 Chequamegon Point

☐ Visited on

_____

Established: (1868) 1896
Status: Inactive/ruins
Location: (WI) West end of Long Island
Type: Pyramidal steel/skeletal
Access: Boat
About the Light: *Rebuilt the same year as La Pointe Light, and receiving the old lens from that light, this light was also under the control of the La Pointe keeper. This 42-foot-tall structure was recently replaced by a modern "light on a post," but the historic light was left standing. Erosion by Lake Superior also threatened the light and it has been moved 50 yards inland to a more protected position. This light is located on a small island in the lake and can be accessed only by boat.*

38 La Pointe

☐ Visited on

_____

Established: (1858) 1896
Status: Active
Location: (WI) Northeast edge of Long Island
Type: Skeletal
Access: Boat
About the Light: *This light marks the east side of the North Channel out of Chequamegon Bay. The light is an iron skeletal structure that stands 65 feet tall. In 1964 the light was automated and the original optic was replaced with a 300mm plastic lens. At least one source says that this was an airport style beacon. The site is a part of the Apostle Islands National Seashore and is open to the public and accessed by use of local tour-boats.*

39 Michigan Island (First Light)

☐ Visited on

_____

Established: 1857
Status: Inactive
Location: (WI) Michigan Island, southeast end
Type: Conical, rough stone
Access: Boat
About the Light: *Deactivated in 1929, this tower stands 64 feet tall. This site is under the protection of the National Park Service, and is in very good condition. The lighthouse is open to the public from June through August. Access is gained by any of a number of local tour-boats from the mainland cities of Ashland or Bayfield.*

40 Michigan Island (Second Light)

☐ Visited on
_____

Established: 1929
Status: Active
Location: (WI) 100 feet from the first tower
Type: Skeletal
Access: Boat
About the Light: *Standing 112 feet tall, the skeletal tower dates from 1880 was disassembled and moved to this site in 1929. This light's original optic was replaced by a rotating "airport type" beacon in 1975 and the original lens is now on display at Apostle Island National Park headquarters in Bayfield. Both this and the first light were intended to guide traffic in and out of Bayfield and Ashland. An excursion boat from the mainland at Ashland can take you to the island.*

41 Raspberry Island

☐ Visited on
_____

Established: 1863
Status: Inactive
Location: (WI) Southwest tip of the island
Type: Square/integral wooden tower and dwelling
Access: Boat
About the Light: *Being wood-framed, this lighthouse has survived well considering that it was deactivated in 1957 when the light was moved to a nearby metal tower The original lens is now on display at Madeline Island Historical Museum. The site is under the supervision of the National Park Service and is open to the public from June through August by means of tour-boat access.*

42 Outer Island

☐ Visited on
_____

Established: 1874
Status: Active
Location: (WI) Northeast end of Outer Island
Type: Conical brick tower and attached dwelling
Access: Boat
About the Light: *The 60 year old keeper of this light, John Irvine, heroically rescued crew members from the schooner-barge PRETORIA which wrecked near the light in 1905. The light itself is one of the Poe styled towers with an adjacent keepers residence. This location is on the outer most of the cluster of the Apostle Islands. Automated in 1961, the tower stands 90 feet tall and today shines a solar-powered light.*

43 Devils Island

☐ Visited on

_____

Established: (1891) 1901*
Status: Active
Location: (WI) North tip of the island
Type: Skeletal
Access: Boat

About the Light: *This light marks the spot where lakeboats running in and out of the ports of Duluth and Superior change course to line up with those ports on the cross-lake track. It stands 82 feet tall and has a range of more than 20 miles. Like all of the lights in the Apostle Islands, this one is under the control of the National Park Service and is open to the public from June through August and accessed by tour-boat.*

*Although the tower was ready in the fall of 1898, there was a three year delay in supplying it with a lens.

44 Sand Island

☐ Visited on

_____

Established: 1881
Status: Active
Location: (WI) Northeast tip of Sand Island
Type: Octagonal/integral brownstone
Access: Boat

About the Light: *A twin to the Eagle Harbor light to the east, and the White River lighthouse over on Lake Michigan, this light was automated in 1921, deactivated in 1933 and reactivated in 1980. This light is open to the public and in care of the National Park Service. On September 12, 1885, Sand Island Lightkeeper Charles Lederlee spotted the wooden steamer PRUSSIA burning and making a dash for the island. Keeper Lederlee took to his rowboat and pulled through the stormy weather to the rescue of the boat's crew.*

45 Wisconsin Point (Superior South)

☐ Visited on

_____

Established: 1913
Status: Active
Location: (WI) Superior entrance, south breakwater, Port of Superior
Type: Round/integral reinforced concrete
Access: Foot

About the Light: *This is an active aid to navigation and is not open to the public. The port of Superior, Wisconsin is one of the primary shipping points for taconite pellets. Originally, Superior had five massive ore loading docks that were all used around the clock. Today only one is used, but there is still plenty of traffic. This light stands 56 feet tall and has a focal plane of 70 feet above the lake's surface.*

46 Minnesota Point Ruins

☐ Visited on

_____

Established: 1856
Status: Ruins
Location: (MN) North side of Superior entry
Type: Conical, brick
Access: Foot
About the Light: *You have to cross onto Minnesota Point over on the Duluth side and travel south on Minnesota Avenue to find the crumbling remains of this light. The light itself was erected in 1856 as an effort to keep up with the boom in shipping following* the opening of the lock at the Soo. At that time, the only access behind Minnesota Point was through the Superior entry. When the Duluth Ship Canal was opened in 1872, the citizens of Superior feared that it would spell the end of navigation into their town. They were wrong, but Superior did seem to get second best in the waterway improvements from then on. The light was abandoned in 1913.

47 Duluth Harbor North Pier

☐ Visited on

_____

Established: 1910
Status: Active
Location: (MN) End of the Duluth Ship Canal north pier
Type: Conical, cast iron
Access: Foot
About the Light: *Like the other Duluth lights, this one is readily accessible. The visitor can stroll out to the end of the concrete pier, and right up to the light itself. The tower is not open to public access, but you may want to bring a lawn chair along,* because it is a great place to sit and watch the lake go by.

48 Duluth Harbor South ☐ Visited on
Breakwater Outer

_____

Established: (1874) 1901
Status: Active
Location: (MN) End of the south pier of the Ship Canal
Type: Square/integral, brick and cast iron
Access: Foot
About the Light: *Within walking distance of the "Inner" light, is this, the "outer" light. Although the building itself is not open to the public, the site is readily accessible and you can walk right out on the pier and up to the light. The tower stands 35 feet tall and produced a focal plane of 44 feet above Lake Superior. The inner and outer lights comprise a range.*

49 Duluth Harbor South Breakwater Inner

Established: (1889) 1901
Status: Active
Location: (MN) South pier, Duluth Ship Canal
Type: Skeletal, cast iron
Access: Foot
About the Light: *The only place on the lakes where you can visit three distinct types of lights – skeletal, conical and square/integral – all in one place within walking distance of one another is* right here. *In fact, if you are handy with a camera it is possible to get all three types of lights in the same photo! The first of these is this one, the Duluth South Breakwater Inner. The light stands 67 feet tall and is of the skeletal type. Access is as simple as parking at the Canal Park Museum and walking across the aerial lift bridge.*

50 Two Harbors

Established: 1892
Status: Active; museum
Location: (MN) On the point between Agate and Burlington bays
Type: Square/integral, brick
Access: Car
About the Light: *Access is gained by exiting off US 61 at 7th Street and head toward the lake. Hang a* left on First Street and a right at 3rd street. Follow that street to the light. The light itself *is an active navigation aid, a museum and a bed and breakfast. Operated by the Lake County Historical Society, the site is in very good hands.*

51 Two Harbors East Breakwater

Established: 1897
Status: Active
Location: (MN) End of breakwater
Type: Pyramidal steel/skeletal
Access: Car
About the Light: *Two Harbors remains a major shipping point for iron ore and taconite pellets.*

· ·

52 Split Rock

☐ Visited on

_____

Established: 1910
Status: Inactive
Location: (MN) 20 miles northeast of Two Harbors
Type: Octagonal Brick
Access: Car
About the Light: *Standing on a bluff, this beautiful brick lighthouse is one of the best looking sights that the lighthouse buff can behold on the lakes. The tower itself is only 54 feet tall, but the elevation of the bluff gives the lamp a focal plane of 168 feet above the lake! Managed by the Minnesota Historical Society, the light has been restored to its pre-1924 appearance. Access is gained by following US 61 to the Split Rock State Park, of which the light is a part. It is open to the public in the summer months, as is the gift shop. The light was decommissioned in 1969.*

53 Grand Marais

☐ Visited on

_____

Established: 1922 (1885)
Status: Active
Location: (MN) End of east breakwater
Type: Pyramidal steel/skeletal
Access: Car
About the Light: *This tower stands just 34 feet tall and has a focal plane of 48 feet. The site is an active aid to navigation and is not open to the general public. It is located adjacent to the local navigation/maritime museum. Access is gained by driving along US-61. The light is constructed upon the harbor's east breakwall and marks the entrance to the harbor.*

54 Rock of Ages

☐ Visited on

_____

Established: 1909
Status: Active
Location: (MI) Off west end of Isle Royale
Type: Conical/bottle-shaped
Access: Boat
About the Light: *Part of the Isle Royale National Park, as well as being an active aid to navigation, this tower stands 130 feet tall and saved many a mariner from the dangers of the sharp rocks off the island. To access the light, you must take the ferry from Grand Portage, MN, to Isle Royale.*

55 Menagerie (Isle Royale)

☐ Visited on

Established: 1875
Status: Active
Location: (MI) On Menagerie Island 20 miles west of Rock Harbor
Type: Octagonal, rough stone and dwelling
Access: Boat
About the Light: *This light is a part of the National Park and is an active aid to navigation. The Island itself is a part of the rough coast line of Isle Royale, and now does more to mark Siskwit Bay than to warn the big oreboats.*

56 Rock Harbor

☐ Visited on

Established: 1855
Status: Inactive; museum
Location: (MI) West end of Rock Harbor
Type: Conical, rough stone and dwelling
Access: Boat
About the Light: *Standing 50 feet tall, this light marked the southeast side of Isle Royale. Although abandoned in 1879, this light was restored by the U.S. Park Service. Today it is used as a museum. To get here, you must take the ferry from Rock Harbor Lodge. Most tourists come via the ferry out of Copper Harbor and Houghton Michigan, but access is also available from Grand Portage, Minnesota. Tour-boats also sail around Isle Royale itself and visit the local lights.*

57 Passage Island

☐ Visited on

Established: 1882
Status: Active
Location: (MI) Southwest end of Passage Island
Type: Octagonal, rough stone and dwelling
Access: Boat
About the Light: *Similar to the White River and Sand Island lights, this lighthouse is made of stone and has a 44-foot-tall tower. It marks a critical point to vessel traffic heading in and out of the Thunder Bay area, and is not open to the public.* However, ferry excursions are available from Rock Harbor Lodge on Isle Royale.

58 Thunder Bay Main

Visited on _____

Established: 1937
Status: Active
Location: (ONT) North breakwater
Type: Square/ integral, wooden tower and dwelling
Access: Boat
About the Light: *This wooden structure gives the appearance of being placed in a temporary location. Its wooden foundation is balanced upon two steel "I" beams that are poised upon four concrete forms. By Lake Superior standards, it seems as if this structure will blow away in the next big gale! The structure has taken the worst of Lake Superior for six decades and remains intact.*

59 Trowbridge Island

Visited on _____

Established: 1910
Status: Active
Location: (ONT) Highest point of this small island
Type: Octagonal, reinforced concrete
Access: Boat
About the Light: *The light marks the eastern approach to Thunder Bay.*

60 Porphyry Point

Visited on _____

Established: 1873
Status: Active
Location: (ONT) Southern tip of Edward Island at the entrance to Black Bay
Type: Skeletal
Access: Boat
About the Light: *This is an active light and is not open to the public. The site is a marking point for traffic in and out of Thunder Bay. Standing 48 feet tall the light does as much service today as it did in 1873. The site is accessible by boat, but the safest way to see it is probably by air.*

61 Shaganash Island

☐ Visited on

_____

Established: 1910
Status: Active
Location: (ONT) West of Shaganash Island on Island #10
Type: Pyramidal, wooden tower
Access: Boat/seaplane
About the Light: *Isolation and a rugged landscape are the char-acteristics of this light. The tower, which helps to mark the isolated inside passage along the North Channel, stands 24 feet tall and is an active aid to navigation. The best way to visit this light is by the use of a boat or an aircraft.*

62 Battle Island

☐ Visited on

_____

Established: (1877) 1911
Status: Active
Location: (ONT) Southeast end of Battle Island
Type: Octagonal; reinforced concrete
Access: Boat
About the Light: *One of the northern most lights on the lakes, this light is one of the most remote sites as well. Standing 44 feet tall, the tower is made of whitewashed brick. When automated in 1991, this light was the last on the lakes staffed by an actual "light keeper," but many lights on Lake Michigan and some on Lake Huron are still manned by Coast Guard staff who do the basic job of keepers. The light is now open to the public at the discretion of the last keeper, Mr. Bert Saasto, who still lives there.*

63 Slate Islands

☐ Visited on

_____

Established: 1902
Status: Active
Location: (ONT) Southwest end of Patterson Island
Type: Octagonal; wooden tower
Access: Boat
About the Light: *Slate Islands comprise a group of 17 islands and inlets in the northeast corner of Lake Superior, approxi-mately 10 kilometers south of the town of Terrace Bay. The islands have been extensively logged and prospected for gold. The largest herd of caribou remaining on the lake is located here.*

64 Otter Island

☐ Visited on

_____

Established: 1903
Status: Active
Location: (ONT) 137 miles north, northwest of
Sault Saint Marie
Type: Octagonal; wooden tower
Access: Boat
About the Light: *In the author's opinion, this IS the most remote light on the lakes. Located on an island just off the Canadian mainland, the site is in the most isolated part of Lake Superior. From here it takes a long time to fly to civilization, let alone sail there. The light stands atop a tree-carpeted rock and remains an active navigation site. It is not open to the public, and if you find yourself here... you are probably shipwrecked.*

65 Devleaux Island

☐ Visited on

_____

Established: (1872) 1911
Status: Active
Location: (ONT) South side of Michipicoten Island
Type: Octagonal; reinforced concrete
Access: Boat
About the Light: *Just below Michipicoten Island, this light is located atop a sliver of land and marks the south side. It is the only indication of civilization in the area. The light is not open to the public.*

66 Michipicoten Island (East End)

☐ Visited on

_____

Established: 1912
Status: Active
Location: (ONT) Southeast end of the island
Type: Hexagonal; reinforced concrete with flying buttresses!
Access: Boat
About the Light: *Standing 71 feet tall this light plays the important role of marking the east end of the island to traffic heading in and out of Whitefish Bay. The light is not open to the public, and the island's very remote location would keep away all but the most enthusiastic light buffs. It remains one of only five flying-buttress-style lights still in service across all of Canada.*

67 Caribou Island

☐ Visited on

_____

Established: 1912
Status: Active
Location: (ONT) Shoal southwest of Caribou Island
Type: Hexagonal; reinforced concrete with 6 flying buttresses
Access: Boat
About the Light: *A near twin to the Michipicoten Island light, this light stands 82 feet tall. Some sources state that this is the area near where the EDMUND FITZGERALD grounded prior to her sinking... it is not. The FITZ allegedly hit Chummy Bank's six fathom shoal which is seven and one half miles due north of this light and on the other side of Caribou Island. The light is an active aid to navigation and is not open to the public. It remains one of only five flying-buttress-style lights still in service across all of Canada.*

68 Coppermine Point

☐ Visited on

_____

Established: 1910
Status: Inactive
Location: (ONT) 55 miles north of Sault Ste. Marie on Hwy 17
Type: Pyramidal; wooden tower
Access: Car
About the Light: *The light was moved to its present site, part of a restaurant complex, when decomissioned.*

69 Ile Parisienne

☐ Visited on

_____

Established: 1912
Status: Active
Location: (ONT) Southwest end of Isle Parisienne
Type: Octagonal; reinforced concrete
Access: Boat
About the Light: *This light is in one of the areas of very high volume traffic on the Great Lakes. Upbound and downbound lakeboats and lake-visiting salties all pass this area on their way in and out of Lake Superior. Although close to the Soo, the waters around this area can be more than 400 feet deep! The light tower stands 30 feet tall and is not open to the public because it is an active and very critical aid to navigation.*

70 Gros Cap Reef

☐ Visited on
_____

Established: 1962
Status: Active
Location: (ONT) Southern Whitefish Bay
Type: Reinforced concrete and steel
Access: Boat
About the Light: *The unique feature of this light is its shape. The concrete crib that supports the light has a plow shape to help fend off the ice flows and storm waves of the big lake. This light made the U.S. light at Point Iroquois obsolete. Located adjacent to the main shipping channel in an area of very high traffic volume, it marks the head of the St. Marys River system, and is a major calling-in point for both upbound and downbound river traffic.*

Keeper Smith's
Housewarming

Lake Superior's coast is a hostile place and it has always been that way. Granted there are some select days when the big lake takes a break from her freezing temper tantrums, but those times are few in number. In the summer when the low gray sky opens to blue and the winds hold their screams, the locals and tourists can take some time to enjoy the elegance of the big lake. But, when the storm winds come calling the fury of the freshwater sea is something that only a native of the Superior coast can admire, and that is best done from a close proximity to a roaring fireplace. Even in modern times, it is true that along most of the Lake Superior coast, neither man nor beast wants to be caught out in the open when the lake kicks up a gale. One such spot along the coast is Grand Island. Squatting just outside of the harbor of Munising, Michigan, Grand Island is a massive rock outcrop that was left behind by the receding ice age glacier that created the Great Lakes. Jutting 175 feet tall, the big island provides a natural shelter for the harbor of Munising, and a good spot for the establishment of a lighthouse.

In the year 1856, a lighthouse was opened on the north side of Grand Island. The first locks at Sault Saint Marie had opened the previous year, and in anticipation of the navigation boom to come the lighthouse board had squeezed a few dollars from their budget for the construction of a few lights on Lake Superior. A spartan sum of $5,000 had been shelled out for the construction of the Grand Island light, and construction was finished in 1856. There is some conflict in the date for the light's birth and on occasion the year 1854 is given. Often the term "established" is quite flexible in the history of lighthouses, meaning, "funded," "started construction," "opened and activated" or all of the above. The odds are that the station's construction was started in 1854, but it was activated in 1856.

"Seen here, the wood-framed Grand Island East Channel lighthouse is probably quite similar to Keeper Smith's original Grand Island North light of 1856."

To Keeper Ruben Smith it meant little; he had a lighthouse and that was all that mattered. Keeper Smith's lighthouse was made of the most economical and available construction material at hand – lumber. There are no pictures of the 1856 lighthouse, but it is a good bet to say that it was similar to the Grand Island East light which, although dilapidated, stands today. It was likely a schoolhouse style structure with a square tower. Standing atop the tall island cliff, the light probably had a focal plane of more than 200 feet and could likely be seen for some 30 or more miles in clear weather. Although isolated, Keeper Smith's light was easily found.

We can only imagine what the remoteness of the Superior shore was like on the next to last day of October, 1856 when the 191 foot sidewheel steamer SUPERIOR ran head-on into one of the big lake's tantrums. The boat was bound for the city of Superior, Wisconsin from Chicago, but some of her passengers that survived would thankfully find themselves as guests at Keeper Smith's lighthouse.

Along with the opening of the "State Locks" at the Soo, vessel traffic finally had ready access to the expanse of Lake Superior. Prior to 1855, the only vessels of substantial size on Lake Superior had to be portaged around the Saint

Marys Rapids. This meant that the hulls of the boats had to be dragged ashore and then hauled across dry land using rolling logs and skids to a point above the rapids where they were returned to the water. Once in the upper river, the boats were land-locked on Lake Superior and whatever cargoes that they were con-signed to carry had to also be portaged around the rapids. Even in modern times, the road that runs along the riverbank at the Soo is called "Portage Avenue." The result of all of this portaging was that the rich minerals of iron ore and copper that existed in the Lake Superior region could only be shipped in barrels that were small enough to be portaged. Thus, the expense of shipping prohibited the mining and use of these raw materials. As soon as the locks at the Soo were opened, a mad dash of lake vessels rushed onto Lake Superior and the local economies boomed. Along with the rush of vessel traffic came a rush to estab-lish navigation aids, such as lighthouses. With great haste, lights were erected at Point Iroquois, Rock Harbor, Minnesota Point, Eagle Harbor, Portage River and Grand Island.

Among the lakeboats in the rush was the steamer SUPERIOR. As with many vessels of her ilk, this big side-wheeler had spent many decades hauling passengers and cargo around the lower lakes. By 1856, the SUPERIOR was only in her 11th season of service and was relatively young by Great Lakes standards when she found herself engaged in sailing across her namesake lake. Passing through the Soo locks late on Tuesday, October 28th 1856, the boat made a brief stop at that same city before pressing onto Lake Superior the following morn-ing. Vessels such as the SUPERIOR, were the best, and often the only form of transportation around the northern wilderness and every time that she put her lines to a pier there were passengers and cargo to be exchanged. As the big side-wheeler transitioned through the Soo, everyone knew too well that with the sea-son growing late, the gales and ice would soon put a stop to vessel traffic leav-ing only the dog-sled as transportation until April or May. Every square foot of the SUPERIOR's hull would be packed with cargo as she departed Sault Saint Marie. Just how many people were aboard the boat is a question that will never be answered completely. Most sources say that the passengers and crew combined for a number of souls on board in the 40s, but at least one source says there were more than 70 people on the vessel. The exact records of who and how many were aboard remain lost forever.

On the same morning as the SUPERIOR steamed from the Soo, 110 miles to the west on Grand Island, Keeper Smith was attending to the routine chores of his new lighthouse. The weather was pleasant that Wednesday morning, but by mid-day, Lake Superior's winter breath began to blow. From the northwest a thundering gale came roaring and with it the temperatures plummeted, the snow blew and the seas became mountains. Through the night, Keeper Smith kept his light shinning, and the lake continued its tantrum. Friday night was a continuation of the gale, but dawn on Saturday brought a shift of wind to off shore and the tempest died. Early that same morning, two local Indians came calling at the lighthouse and told of a shipwrecked people down on the lake. Immediately, Keeper Smith struck out through the six inch deep snow in quest of the castaways. After a mile hike, the keeper and the two Indians came upon a group of half a dozen near frozen survivors. They told him that more people had been left behind and might still be alive. Keeper Smith directed the group to the light and then headed out toward those left behind. He later discovered two men and a boy, three miles farther away. The boy was dead and the two men were just waiting for the reaper to arrive for them. Instead of the angel of death, Keeper Smith arrived and escorted them to the safety of his lighthouse. These were the survivors of the once proud steamer SUPERIOR.

After departing the Soo, the SUPERIOR was steaming into mild conditions until just before midnight. Suddenly, Lake Superior lashed out at her namesake and showed a rage in which the steamer was never designed to operate. Wallowing in the giant seas and blinded by the snow, the big side-wheeler was completely overpowered and it would not be long before something had to give. The "give" came in the form of the boat's 12-foot-tall oak rudder being ripped from its station. Without the ability to steer the boat was at the mercy of the storm. For hours she drifted, rolling madly in the trough of the seas while the passengers waited in cold terror for the end to come. The boat's smokestacks were knocked over the side by boarding waves and the cattle that were a part of her cargo went insane. After two hours of torment, the cry of "Rocks! Rocks!" was heard just before the boat was slammed into the Michigan shoreline. Crushed between the giant seas and the rugged cliffs of the Pictured Rocks shoreline, the SUPERIOR began to crumble like a paper hat. In short order, the lake had completely shattered the entire vessel and taken her people into her frigid grip. Death came quickly for some, but slowly for others. One survivor reported watching as people who had taken refuge atop the remains of the boat's big paddle wheels, dropped one by one into the sea as the cold overcame their desire to live. Others, who were lucky enough to find the rocks, managed also to capture the steamer's lifeboats. After nearly two days of soaking cold, the waves went down enough to allow them to row for the only point of civilization that they could see – Grand Island and Keeper Smith's lighthouse.

Accounts vary as to how many survivors escaped the lake that day. Some say less than 18 souls lived through the disaster, while others say that the number was more like 23. One group managed to find Keeper Smith, and the comfort of his lighthouse. Without regard to exact figures, Lake Superior had, for the first time, demonstrated that the big fine steamers that now invaded her via the Soo Locks, would never be a match for her true power. From that time on, the lake would always set her sights on the biggest and finest of the lakeboats that would sail her waters.

For a number of days after the wreck, Lighthouse Keeper Smith gave warmth and shelter to his gaggle of survivors. All were suffering to a great extent from frostbite and frozen feet. All were starving and most were in shock. There are indications that more survivors found the lighthouse after the first group. In one account it is stated that they found their way to the "East Channel Lighthouse," but that lighthouse did not exist until 1866, nearly a decade after the SUPERIOR's wreck. Thus it is likely that the light in question was Keeper

Smith's lighthouse. For Smith himself, it was a heavy load to handle, while trying to keep his light working he also had to see to the care of his guests. Then again, this was the first excitement at the lighthouse. Sort of a housewarming of disaster.

As it turned out, the wooden lighthouse on Grand Island was no match for Lake Superior either. In 1867, the old wooden light was so dilapidated that the Lighthouse Board saw fit to replace it with a new brick and stone structure which still stands today. It is currently a private residence having been deactivated in 1961. When the new light opened in 1867, Ruben Smith was named as its keeper and was able to carry on his duty from the original light. In those first few seasons, when the winds howled and the lake raged, it is doubtless that Keeper Smith carried thoughts as to whether or not he would again have housewarming guests

SOURCES

Inland Waters List of Lights, Buoys and Fog Signals, 1995, Canadian Coast Guard

National Park Service 1994 Inventory of Historic Lighthouses

Great Lakes Lighthouses, Roberts and Jones

The Northern Lights, Hyde

Great American Light-houses, Holland

A Traveler's Guide To 100 Eastern Great Lakes Lighthouses, Penrose

A Traveler's Guide To 116 Western Great Lakes Lighthouses, Penrose

A Traveler's Guide To 116 Michigan Lakes Lighthouses, Penrose

Shipwrecks of Lake Huron, Parker

Ghost Ships of the Great Lakes, Boyer

Shipwreck! Swayze

Great Lakes Ships We Remember [Vol.1], Van der Linden

Lake Carriers, Les Strang

Queen of the Lakes, Thompson

Phone conversation with Seaman Thomas Prisco, USCG Tawas Point Station 6/12/1997

Great Lakes Cruiser magazine, Nov. 1994 *"The Old Lighthouse at Presque Isle"* Ken Miller

A Pictorial History of the Great Lakes, Hatcher & Walter

Georgian Bay, An Illustrated History, Barry

Dive Ontario!, Kohl

Dive Ontario Two!, Kohl

Lake Ontario, Pound

Lake Erie, Hatcher

Lake Huron, Landon

Lake Michigan, Quaife

Lake Superior, Nute

Annual Report of the Operations of the Light-House Board, all volumes used from 1852, 1864 through 1912

Lighthouse Digest, Aug. 1995 *"A Visit to Michigan's Presque Isle Light"* Harrison

Lighthouse Digest, Aug. 1995 *"Big Red Lighthouse... Off Limits?,"* Harrison

Lighthouse Digest, Aug. 1995 *"The Lost Lights of Racine,"* Harrison

Shipwrecks of the Straits of Mackinac, Feltner

Phone Conversation with Richard Moehl, President, Great Lakes Lighthouse Keepers Association, 7/11/1997

The Unholy Apostles, Keller

Point Beach State Forest welcome guide.

Author's visit to Rawley Point lighthouse, 9/1/1994

"Observations," The Noreaster, May/June 1997

Dangerous Coast, Stonehouse, Fountain

Oswego Daily Palladium, 9/26/1921

Ice Water Museum, Oleszewski

Ghost Ships, Gales and Forgotten Tales, Oleszewski

Conversation with Cdr. Griff Hamilton, USN Retired 8/1992

Bay City Daily Tribune, 9/3,13/1881, 11/14,16/1883

Bay City Evening Press, 9/27,28,30/1881

The Bay of Dead Ships, Reich

E-mail from Dan Fountain, Great Lakes Historian/Author 9/20/1997

GREAT LAKES LIGHTHOUSES

188

Index, Lighthouses by Lake

189

GREAT LAKES LIGHTHOUSES

LAKE SUPERIOR

Index, Lighthouses by State

GREAT LAKES LIGHTHOUSES

· ·

GREAT LAKES LIGHTHOUSES

ABOUT THE AUTHOR

Wes Oleszewski was born on the east-side of Saginaw, Michigan in 1957. Through most of his youth Wes kept a passing interest in the vessels of the Great Lakes that was second only to his fascination with the space program and areas of aviation. When accepted for enrollment at the Embry-Riddle Aeronautical University in 1977, Wes' career turned toward aviation leaving room in his life for a diversion deeper into Great Lakes maritime history. Such diversion was often needed during the ten years that were required for him to earn his way through the university. By 1987 Wes had earned a Bachelor of Science Degree in Aeronautical Science with pilot certification through commercial pilot with multi-engine instrument rating.

In the summer of 1986, Wes was earning money to return to school by working days as a film delivery driver and nights as a part-time clerk at Land and Seas gift shop, at that time in Saginaw. While there he noticed that every book on the shelf was already in his own personal library. With that in mind Wes sat down the next day during his lunch hour and began writing his first book on a legal pad. No one ever told him how it was done – and better yet – no one ever told him that he couldn't do it. For the next year he assembled the true stories of the obscure adventures of the lake mariners, the tales that everyone else had overlooked. Over the summer of 1987, while Wes attended classes in a doubled effort to graduate, his soon-to-be wife Teresa transferred the hand written text into computer text. That same summer Wes sent the text off to a well-known Great Lakes publisher, who promptly rejected it. In 1990 the exact same text was sent to Avery – who promptly published it as *Stormy Seas*.

Since that first book hit the shelf, Wes has written and Avery has published *Sounds of Disaster, Ice Water Museum* and *Ghost Ships, Gales and Forgotten Tales* and *Mysteries and Histories: Shipwrecks of the Great Lakes.* Wes has written more than a quarter of a million words about the mariners of the Great Lakes. Currently Wes has more than 40 stories in research and can produce a book every year. He is busy at work on his sixth book of true life Great Lakes Shipwreck adventures and a book of the true adventures of the Great Lakes Lighthouses as well. Aside from writing and working at his other job as an airline pilot, Wes finds time to travel around the Great Lakes region visiting book stores to sign copies of his work, researching local maritime history, and his favorite side-trip… speaking to classrooms of students from the elementary level up. Often the enthusiastic boat-nut can find Wes perched on the canal wall at Duluth, shooting video tape under the bridge at Port Huron or hanging out on the west observation platform at the Soo locks… like most professional pilots, he gets around.

As of this publication Wes has logged more that 5,000 hours of flying time, most of that in airline category aircraft, but has recently found a home flying his first love in aviation: the Falcon Jet. As his wife and friends can attest to, other than writing, Wes is only happy when flying higher, farther and faster, and the Falcon Jet's speed of 84% of the speed of sound suits him just fine… for now. Currently, he holds the highest pilot certification issued by the FAA, the Airline Transport Pilot certificate, and has achieved the rank of airline captain. He is presently living on the east coast and employed as a pilot for an international VIP charter company.

ABOUT THE PHOTOGRAPHER

Photographer Wayne S. Sapulski focuses on nautical themes relevant to the Great Lakes, around which he has travelled extensively by both land and sea. Wayne's articles and photographs have appeared in a number of regional publications and art shows. A graduate of the Great Lakes Maritime Academy, Wayne served as a USCG Licensed Deck Officer aboard several of the large freighters that ply the lakes. Still licensed but no longer sailing, Wayne remains active in a number of maritime historical societies and lighthouse groups, especially the Great Lakes Lighthouse Keepers Association (GLLKA). Wayne's goal, almost completed, remains to personally visit and photograph every remaining light station on the Great Lakes. A native of southeastern Michigan, Wayne resides in Plymouth, Michigan.

Other Avery Color Studios, Inc. publications by Wes Oleszewski are:

- *Stormy Disasters*

- *Ice Water Museum*

- *Ghost Ships, Gales & Forgotten Tales*

- *Mysteries and Histories,*
  Shipwrecks of the Great Lakes

- *Lighthouse Adventures,*
  Heroes, Haunts & Havoc On The Great Lakes

- *Keepers of Valor, Lakes of Vengeance,*
  Lakeboats, Lifesavers & Lighthouses

Avery Color Studios, Inc. has a full line of Great Lakes oriented books, puzzles, cookbooks, shipwreck and lighthouse maps, lighthouse posters and Fresnel lens model.

For a free full-color catalog, call **1-800-722-9925**.

> Avery Color Studios, Inc. products are available at gift shops and bookstores throughout the Great Lakes region.